Choosing Childcare:
A Guide for Parents and Providers

Ann Mooney and
Anthony G. Munton

with illustrations by
Philip Hopman

arena

© Ann Mooney and Anthony G. Munton 1997

Published by
Arena
Ashgate Publishing Limited
Gower House
Croft Road
Aldershot
Hants GU11 3HR
England

Ashgate Publishing Company
Old Post Road
Brookfield
Vermont 05036
USA

British Library Cataloguing in Publication Data
Mooney, Ann
   Choosing childcare : a guide for parents and providers
   1. Child care services – Great Britain
   I. Title   II. Munton, Anthony G.   III. Hopman, Philip
   362. 7'12'0941

Library of Congress Catalog Card Number: 96-85242

ISBN 1 85742 361 5

Typeset in Goudy by Raven Typesetters, Chester
and printed and bound in Great Britain
by The University Press, Cambridge

Contents

Acknowledgements

The authors would like to thank the following people for their very valuable comments on earlier drafts of the manuscript: Ann Barry, Margaret Bowen, Amanda Hoskins, Sarah Lilley, Laraine McKeon, Carole Mrozek, Sonja Schwartz, June Statham and Shelagh Waugh.

Introduction

It is a fact that more and more people are using childcare and preschool services for their young children. Nine out of every ten children in England have been in non-parental care of some sort before starting school. As more and more parents use childcare, so the demand for places continues to grow, largely because of a rise in the numbers of women in paid work who have young children. More mothers have jobs today than at any other time since the end of the Second World War. By 1991, nearly half of all mothers with a child under 5 were in paid work. By the year 2000, it is estimated that 80 per cent of new jobs will be taken by women returning to work. Most mothers have part-time jobs, but this is also changing. More women returning to work are going back into full-time jobs.

Mothers are returning to work after having a child for three reasons: financial necessity, career development or personal choice.

- *Financial necessity:* Having a child can cost a family a lot of money. It's not just the expense of a new member of the family, there's also the drop in income if a parent stops working. Women often don't have much choice about going back to work: many families cannot make ends meet without their income. For single parents, the situation is even more difficult.

- *Career development:* Two out of every three women who return to work after a break to have children go back part-time. Almost half return to a lower-grade job than the one they had before. Taking a break from work to bring up children can damage a woman's career development.

- *Personal choice:* Some women are content to stop working and be at home with their young children. Other women find staying at home full-time less satisfying. Obviously, mothers who choose to work do not love their children any less: it is just that they are likely to be happier if they go back to work rather than stay at home. Feeling positive about what you choose to do is a very important part of building a successful relationship with your child. It is much better for a child to spend a few hours a day with a mother who goes out to work and is happy about it than all day with a mother who resents being at home.

Of course, going to work is not the only reason parents use childcare: they may be studying or training, they may want a little time for themselves, or they may want their child to mix with other children.

The increased demand for childcare has been met almost entirely by private nursery-owners and childminders. Between 1988 and 1994, the number of private nurseries almost doubled; the number of places with registered childminders more than doubled. Meanwhile, the number of places in publicly-funded (council) nurseries has shrunk. Now less than 10 per cent of children have a publicly-funded place in a council nursery.

Does this mean that most of the children of working parents are in formal care, for example with nurseries and childminders? No. Half of all women who go out to work leave their children with grandparents or other relatives. A government survey of mothers working full-time found that 38 per cent were cared for by a grandparent and 12 per cent by another relative. This compared with 21 per cent using childminders, 17 per cent using playgroups and 14 per cent using day nurseries.

Why the need for this book?

Much has been written about the effects of children being cared for outside the home. Picking out the good advice from the bad is not always easy. It is commonly held that young children suffer from being looked after by anyone other than their parents, but research evidence does not support this. Most childcare experts agree that as far as child development is concerned, it doesn't matter whether a child is in the care of a parent or another adult – what counts is that they receive *good quality care*.

Of course, development depends very much on the home life that parents create for their children, but what happens to children outside the home is important too. Experiences in childcare can have a lasting effect on how children get on later in their lives. Good quality childcare can help children from difficult family backgrounds to develop to the best of their abilities. Unfortunately, it is also true that poor quality childcare can undo much of the good work done by parents. In the space of a week, a child in full-time childcare spends as much time with other carers as with their parents. Whether a young child spends a couple of hours or five days a week in childcare, the experience should be beneficial. Good quality childcare can help your child:

- mix better with other children and adults
- learn to talk earlier
- get more out of playing
- learn to share and take turns
- be better behaved
- learn to follow rules and instructions
- settle more quickly into school

When they are choosing a nursery, a playgroup or a childminder for their child, many parents are unsure what they should be looking for. We have written this book to help you make your choice, by discussing what good quality childcare is, and how to spot it.

Who is this book for?

This book is for parents planning to use, or already using, some form of childcare or preschool service for their children. We have written the book for parents who want full-time childcare, but much of the information will be useful for parents seeking part-time care as well. One in three working parents place their children either in day nurseries or with childminders. For this reason, we have chosen to concentrate on looking for good quality nurseries or childminders. However, the same information about quality is relevant to most other kinds of childcare, such as that provided by playgroups, nursery classes, nannies and relatives.

How to find your way around this book

We have divided the book into three parts.

Part one deals with:

- different types of childcare service
- the different needs of parents, children and childcare providers
- choosing the best type of care for your child
- how the law tries to ensure that parents and children obtain good childcare

Part two describes:

- 13 important features of childcare that can help you to decide if a nursery or childminder is offering a good quality service.

Part three discusses:

- the practical problems of finding childcare
- how to find good childminders and nurseries
- how to choose a place that suits you and your child
- how to decide whether the childcare provider offers good quality care
- how to make the arrangement work

Each part of the book includes information boxes which summarize important points.

Definitions of terms

'Childcare' is used to cover all provision available for the under-fives, including day nurseries, childminders, nannies, nursery classes, playgroups and reception classes. We have used 'childcare provider' to describe anyone who provides childcare. When referring to childminders, we have chosen to use the personal pronouns 'she' and 'her'. Although men do work as childminders, sometimes jointly with their partners, it remains the case that most childminders are women.

Part one

Part one of *Choosing Childcare* is about basics. It answers questions that all parents have about leaving their children with other people. It contains four chapters:

- Chapter 1 – What childcare services are available?
- Chapter 2 – What do people need from childcare?
- Chapter 3 – How do you decide what's best for your child?
- Chapter 4 – Good quality childcare and the law

1
What childcare services are available?

There are several different kinds of childcare for children under 5 for you to choose from. We have divided them up into childcare choices that provide mostly full-time care, and those that usually offer only part-time care (see Box 1.1). Places that can take children for only an hour or two at a time are often said to offer 'sessional' care. A 'session' is usually part of a day – from 9.30 a.m. until 11.30 a.m., for example.

Some choices in Box 1.1 may not be available in your area. You will need to do some detective work before making up your mind.

The main differences between the types of care listed in Box 1.1 are:

- the hours they are open
- the number of children they take
- the amount of training staff they have
- the type of service they offer
- the extent to which parents are expected to help
- the cost

Information box 1.1: Childcare choices you may have

Full-time care:

- childminders
- day nurseries
- relatives and friends
- nannies

Part-time (sessional) care:

- playgroups
- parent/carer and toddler groups
- nursery schools
- nursery classes
- reception classes (9.00 a.m.–3.30 p.m.)

We will now deal with each of these childcare and preschool options in more detail. For each option, we have tried to list the factors you may want to consider before making your choice.

Childminders

Childminders are often, but not always, parents themselves. Many childminders start doing the job so that they can combine paid work with looking after their own children. The usual way childminders work is to provide childcare in their own home, for payment. Childminders must work within regulations set out in the 1989 Children Act. *Any childminder who looks after children under the age of 8 for more than two hours a day must be registered with their local authority.* This is the law. You will find a simple guide to the

Children Act in Chapter 4, which also explains why it is so important that parents use only registered childcare providers.

Most childminders offer full-time care, all the year round. Of course, childminders often don't work on public holidays and many take an annual holiday like the rest of us. They provide children with a range of care and play activities in a family setting. As part of their weekly activities, childminders may take children to a playgroup or nursery for a few hours. Some belong to childminding groups, where they take part in activities with other minders and children.

Under the Children Act, local authorities have to make sure that both childminders and their homes are suitable for providing childcare. Childminders don't *have* to have any training or formal qualifications. Nevertheless, more and more childminders today want to be trained. Some local authorities ask anyone wanting to register as a childminder for the first time to take a short training course. Local authorities usually allow (register) childminders to look after no more than three children under the age of 5, including the childminders's own children. In some areas, they do not allow childminders to look after more than one baby under a year old. Childminders often look after school-age children too. This can be a useful service for parents who leave work after their children finish school.

Finding that childminders have more children in their home after school and in the holidays is common. Nevertheless, local authority regulations stipulate that a childminder can look after no more than six children under the age of 8 at a time, including her own children. Of these six, no more than three can be under the age of 5. The cost of childminding varies. They usually charge fees on an hourly, daily, weekly or sessional (morning or afternoon) basis. Some employers, such as Boots, have started schemes which involve them paying towards the cost of childminding for their employees.

Box 1.2 sets out some matters you should consider when deciding whether to use a childminder.

Information box 1.2: Should I choose a childminder?

Things to think about:

- A childminder may live quite near your home.
- A childminder's working hours may be more flexible than a nursery, though they will not be happy if you always arrive earlier or later than agreed.
- A childminder who is ill cannot look after your child.
- Although childminders should not take children who are unwell, they are often willing to look after them if the illness is minor and not infectious.
- Childminders can move or stop working as a childminder.
- On the other hand, childminders are in a better position to offer consistent care beyond school age.
- Their home is not specially designed for children, just as your home isn't, although some childminders do have a play room.

Day nurseries

Most day nurseries are *private*, although local authorities still run some. Private nurseries are usually open all year round, apart from bank holidays and possibly a couple of weeks in the summer, or between Christmas and New Year. Most provide care for children between the ages of 2 and 5. Places for babies tend to be limited. Nurseries vary in size. The smallest we have come across had just ten places. The bigger nurseries usually look after children in smaller groups. In most nurseries, at least some staff are trained in childcare. The number of trained staff varies between nurseries. Nursery fees can be expensive, particularly for children under 2, but this depends on the nursery.

Private nurseries are usually run as a business, but some nurseries are run by *community* or *voluntary organizations*. These nurseries are non-profitmaking. They depend on grants and subsidies from councils and other organizations. Because they don't have to make a profit, community or voluntary nurseries often charge less for a place than private nurseries.

Some offices, factories, hospitals and colleges have opened nurseries for their staff and/or students. These are known as *workplace nurseries*, and they are usually located in or very near the workplace. Employers usually subsidize workplace nurseries. Fees are often lower than in private nurseries. Often the charge will vary depending on how much an employee earns. A group of different companies may pool resources to provide a workplace nursery. Alternatively, an employer may reserve places at a local private nursery. This kind of arrangement has become more popular in the last couple of years. Although workplace nurseries are usually only for children of company employees, some do offer places to non-company parents if they have vacancies. Indeed, some workplace nurseries are set up to offer places to both their employees and the public. For example, Network Southeast have opened nurseries close to railway stations to offer childcare services both to their staff and commuters. However, workplace nurseries are not easy to find, and those that do exist usually have long waiting lists. A recent survey found that nine out of every ten workplace nurseries had a waiting list. What's more, around half of all workplace nurseries are in London and the Southeast. The same survey found that employers were offering reduced fees in two out of three nurseries, but couldn't meet the demand from their own staff for places.

Local authority day nurseries usually only provide places for children they consider to have special educational, psychological or emotional needs. Working conditions for staff are often better in local authority nurseries than in the private sector. Trained staff look after children in smaller groups: that means more staff to each child. The number of local authority nurseries has greatly reduced over recent years. Strict rules for admission mean that most parents are unlikely to be able to send their child to a local authority nursery. However, it might be worth checking with your own town hall. In some areas, local authority day nurseries do have some places reserved for community use.

Local authorities must register most day nurseries. The only exceptions are private schools offering places for both under- and over-fives. Every registered nursery is subject to an annual inspection from the local authority. The nursery must meet particular standards to do with health, safety, space, numbers of children and staff, and the activities available to children.

Box 1.3 gives examples of some things you should consider when deciding whether to send your child to a day nursery.

Montessori

As you look through lists of day nurseries and nursery schools, you will come across some places calling themselves 'Montessori'

**Information box 1.3: Should I choose
a day nursery?**

Things to think about:

- Most nursery premises are purpose-built or specially adapted for children.
- The nursery may close down and staff may leave. It may not offer a stable environment for your child.
- You cannot drop your child off before the nursery is open, and you must collect your child before closing time.
- Apart from very unusual circumstances, the nursery is always available to care for your child.
- Using a workplace nursery may mean that changing your job means losing the nursery place.
- Workplace nurseries may not be near where you live.
- If the nursery is not in your area, you may find it difficult to keep in touch with your child's nursery friends outside nursery hours.
- Many nurseries have long waiting lists, especially for baby places.
- The nursery will not take your child on days they are ill.

---

nurseries. Maria Montessori, an Italian doctor who died in 1952, believed that children have a natural desire to learn. Based on her philosophies, Montessori nurseries aim to provide a carefully structured learning environment. Learning materials and nursery staff encourage children to learn for themselves through self-discovery rather than formal teaching. Parents should still make all the usual checks when it comes to choosing a 'Montessori' nursery. In our experience, some nurseries calling themselves 'Montessori' don't follow the doctor's principles, just as some nurseries who take a child-centred approach don't call themselves 'Montessori.'

Relatives and friends

For many parents, relatives provide care for their children during the day. Things are changing though. The need to move to find work or gain promotion means that it's much less common for families to stay in the same area. Even if families do still live in the same area, it's more likely that relatives will be working themselves and not be available to provide childcare.

It's quite understandable for parents to want a relative or friend to care for their child. There is the advantage that they already know and trust the person. Parents also feel that relatives will make better carers because of their close emotional ties to the child. Nevertheless, it's not always the best option. As any parent will tell you, looking after children full-time is hard work. You need to be physically fit, patient and adaptable to a child's changing needs. Older relatives especially may find looking after a small child too much of a challenge. Health conditions such as heart problems, arthritis or respiratory difficulties would make childcare more demanding. Relatives may not always be happy about changing their routines or moving their furniture around to suit the demands of a young child. Different generations often have different ideas about how to bring up children. Obviously, that can sometimes lead to problems, but some relatives can and do provide excellent childcare.

Relatives may not want you to pay them. You may consider this a decisive factor, but paying relatives for providing care can have its advantages. For one thing, payment makes the arrangement more formal, which can make it easier for you: you can raise matters that may be worrying you, or make your wishes clear about how you want your child cared for. It takes away the feeling that someone is doing you a favour. Payment also sends a message to all concerned that looking after children is a job, which should be rewarded. If a relative insists that they do not want or need the money, you may want to think about other solutions – for example, paying money into a bank account in the child's name might help everyone feel happy with the arrangement.

Close relatives do not have to register with their local authority, but registering as a childminder allows relatives to take in more children should they want to. Also, they may benefit from services that the local authority offers childminders, such as a toy library or drop-in facility.

Very often, friends of the family offer to look after young children. *If a friend provides care for more than two hours a day for payment, they must be registered with the local authority.* Friends who do not register are breaking the law. Registration is not difficult, and can bring advantages. Most important, local authorities strongly recommend that registered childminders be insured to care for children. Just think: what you would do if your child was involved in an accident that meant they needed full-time nursing care for long periods. You could take legal action, but if your friend was not insured how would they afford to pay compensation? And how would you feel about your friend then?

Box 1.4 gives examples of some factors to consider when deciding whether to allow relatives or friends to look after your child.

Information box 1.4: Should I choose a relative or a friend?

Things to think about:

- Relatives can provide a less expensive form of childcare. They do deserve to be paid, however.
- Family relationships and friendships might suffer if you don't see eye-to-eye over something.
- Relatives usually have a special relationship with the child.
- Relatives may be able to help out part-time. You could combine this with another type of care, such as a part-time nursery or playgroup place.
- Family relationships may mean it is difficult to say what you feel about how your child is being looked after.
- If your child is ill, relatives may still be willing to look after them.
- Relatives may be more flexible about hours, particularly drop-off and collection times.

Nannies

Nannies are usually only an option for those with plenty of money. Not surprisingly, this is still the least common form of childcare for the majority of parents. You employ a nanny to come into your home and care for your child. The most common qualification among nannies is the Nursery Nurse Examination Board

certificate (NNEB). However, many nannies have BTec Nursery Nursing or NVQ qualifications. Employing a qualified and experienced nanny can be expensive. As her employer, you may have to deduct her PAYE tax and National Insurance contributions, unless she is self-employed. A nanny does not have to be registered by the local authority. *However, if the nanny is shared by more than two families, the law says they have to be registered.* Sharing a nanny with another family can help to reduce the cost.

One problem about employing a nanny is the fact that few seem to stay long in one job. Nannies often move on after one or two years. Your child might not receive the stability of care they need. Finding a nanny you like, who likes you and your family, and who is willing to stay until the children reach school age is very difficult.

Box 1.5 sets out some points to consider when deciding whether to employ a nanny.

Information box 1.5: Should I choose a nanny?

Things to think about:

- Childcare takes place in your own home — easier for you and your child.
- There are extra costs, such as heating and lighting, because care is carried out in your own home.
- If the nanny is unable to look after your child because of illness, you will have to make alternative arrangements.
- You need to be clear about working conditions and hours. Draw up a contract.
- Your child can have the undivided attention of one adult.
- Stability of care can be a problem. Children can experience several carers in a short space of time.
- The nanny must arrive on time if you are to avoid being late for work (unless they live in).

Playgroups

Playgroups usually take children aged 3 and 4, but some will take 2-year-olds. You will often find more playgroups in areas where there are few local education authority (LEA) nursery classes. Most playgroups are only open during school terms. They usually open for two or three hours in the morning *or* afternoon, but some are open for longer. The number of playgroups offering more hours, or even full-time childcare, is growing. However, most open for five 'sessions' (two or three hours) a week. Playgroups will often limit the number of sessions a week a child can attend. That way, more children are able to use the group. Most children go to playgroups for no more than two or three sessions a week. They will charge you a small fee for each session.

Playgroups are often found in church halls or community centres. They offer a wide range of play and preschool activities. Staff trained in playgroup work usually run them in partnership with parents. Involving parents in the running of the group helps to keep costs down. *By law, local authorities must register playgroups.*

Parent/carer and toddler groups

These groups often meet in places like community centres, health clinics or local halls. They are informal groups, where adults can take young children to play and meet other people. You come and go as you please. There is usually no need to reserve a place. Parent/carer and toddler groups act as a kind of social club. Adults must stay with their child, so you can't use these groups as a childcare option. However, it's quite common to find relatives, childminders or nannies using parent/toddler groups while the parents are at work.

Nursery schools

Nursery schools provide education for children aged around 3–4. They are usually open only during school terms. LEAs provide some, while others are privately run. LEA nursery schools usually offer either morning or afternoon places. Staff, including teachers, are trained, and the provision is free. The Office for Standards in Education (Ofsted) inspects LEA nursery schools every three years.

Private nursery schools are usually only open during school hours, but some do stay open longer for working parents, so it is always worth checking. Fees vary, but can be high. Staff usually include trained teachers. *Private nursery schools must be registered with their local authority.* If they only take children under 5, the local authority will inspect them every year. If the nursery includes children over 5, they must be registered with the Department for Education and Employment, and inspected by Ofsted every three years.

Nursery classes

Nursery classes are usually part of a primary school. Children that go to a nursery class are not always guaranteed a place at the primary school attached to it. Nursery classes offer free, part-time education for children aged 3–4, during term time only. LEAs run nursery classes, and trained teachers and assistants staff them. However, LEAs do not *have* to provide nursery education. Some LEAs provide no nursery education, whereas others guarantee a place for most 4-year-olds in their area. Even if your LEA does provide nursery education, there may not be enough places for every child, so it's important to put your name on the waiting list as soon as possible. If your LEA takes 4-year-olds in reception classes (see below), they will usually offer nursery places to 3-year-olds. You can find out more about what is available in your area by getting in touch with your local education authority.

Reception classes

The law says that children have to start school at the beginning of the first school term after their fifth birthday. However, many LEAs take children into reception classes in primary schools before their fifth birthday. Big cities often have more places in reception classes than smaller towns. The rules for admission to reception classes vary in different areas. For example, some authorities take all children who will be 5 during the school year into reception classes in September. Other authorities take children into classes at the beginning of every term (September, January and April). Usually, places are full-time, that is from 9.00 a.m. until 3.30 p.m. Some children start going to reception classes part-time. Parents do not have to send their child to a reception class just because they are offered a place, but most parents do.

Box 1.6 provides a summary of some of the different childcare and preschool options that might be available in your area.

Childcare costs

There are no standard charges when it comes to childcare. The cost will vary depending on where you live and the type of service you choose. Even within one area, fees for the same kind of care can vary quite a lot. Obviously, supply and demand play a part –

Information box 1.6: Summary of childcare options

	Opening hours	Number of children taken	Staff training	Parental help	Cost
Childminders	Full-time	3 under 5 years old	Not usually required	Not usual	£1–£3.50 per hour
Day nurseries	Full-time	10–70+	Some trained staff (varies)	Not expected	£70–£150 per week
Playgroups	2–3 hours morning or afternoon	10–30	Some trained staff	Usually expected	£1.50–£5 per session
Parent and toddler groups	Once or twice a week	5–20	Not required	Parents stay with children	Nominal charge
Nursery schools	Morning or afternoon during school terms	10–30 per class	Trained teachers and assistants	Not expected	LEA – free; private – average £650 per term
Nursery classes	Morning or afternoon during school terms	20–30	Trained teachers and assistants	Not expected	Free
Reception classes	School hours	Varies – 15–28	Trained teachers and assistants	Not expected	Free

for example, childminders are likely to be more expensive in areas where they are in great demand.

It is often a mistake to think that more expensive childcare means better childcare. You don't always get what you pay for. The cost to you, the parent, can depend on all sorts of things like subsidies, support, profit margins and fees. For example, take day nursery provision. In the private sector, the cost of a nursery place is often very high. This cost has to be met entirely by the fees paid by parents. There are two ways in which the amount that parents pay can be reduced. First, the nursery may receive some kind of grant or support, which can lower fees. Second, the provider may try to reduce their costs. Unfortunately, reducing costs can often mean saving on wages by employing fewer trained staff, or spending less on toys, books or other equipment.

Childcare is expensive. It is no surprise that the first question most parents ask about childcare is 'How much does it cost?' Most parents have to pay. Unlike other European countries, recent British governments have chosen to do very little to help parents with the cost of childcare. Many working mothers pay between a quarter and a half of their take-home pay for childcare. For mothers on low incomes, childcare takes an even bigger proportion of their wages. That makes it more difficult for women in low-paid jobs to go back to work, since they may be no better off financially.

Government help with childcare costs – Childcare Allowance

Families who qualify for Family Credit and some other means-tested benefits can also claim Childcare Allowance. Family Credit is a weekly payment for working families on low wages who have at least one child. Childcare Allowance aims to help people who want to go back to work or work longer hours. From 1 April 1996, the allowance is £60 per family per week. When your income is assessed for Family Credit, Housing Benefit, Council Tax Benefit or Disability Working Allowance, £60 will be disregarded if you are paying for childcare. To qualify, you must use registered childcare and be claiming Family Credit.

For more information about Family Credit, contact your local Citizens' Advice Bureau or the local office of the Department of Social Security.

Employers' help

It is always worth asking your employer if they offer any help with the costs of childcare. Some firms give employees vouchers which they can use towards the cost of childcare. Alternatively, employers may offer low-cost places in a local nursery or workplace nursery. The amount of help you receive with the cost will usually depend on how much you earn. The more you earn, the more you will be expected to pay for the place.

Vouchers for nursery education

In July 1995, the government announced a preschool voucher scheme. Under this scheme, all parents with a 4-year-old child will be eligible to receive vouchers, worth around £1,100 over one year. The government is introducing the scheme in two phases. The first phase began in April 1996, with just four local education authorities testing the scheme. At the time of writing, the government intends all local education authorities to take part from April 1997.

Parents can use the vouchers to pay towards the cost of three terms (one year) of preschool education. They can use their vouchers in any school, nursery, preschool or playgroup allowed to take part in the voucher scheme. To take part, childcare providers must have special permission. This is to assure parents that their children will receive a good standard of education. If the provider fails to meet the standards, they will not be allowed to continue in the scheme.

LEA school reception classes, nursery schools and nursery classes will also require parents of 4-year-olds to hand over their vouchers. Parents will be given a place for their 4-year-old, if there are places available, in exchange for vouchers. You will only get vouchers if you have a child who is 4 years old. In the private and voluntary sectors (for example, playgroups, community nurseries, private day nurseries and nursery schools), vouchers can be used to help pay fees. The following examples give you some idea of how the scheme works.

Jodi will be 4 in the autumn. Since she was 2, she has been going to the day nursery at the company where her dad works. Jodi's parents received a voucher application form in the post from the agency given the job of running the voucher scheme. They completed the form and sent it back to the agency. Having checked that Jodi's parents were eligible, the agency sent them vouchers which they can now use for the autumn term, when Jodi will be 4. Another set of vouchers will be sent for the spring term, and another for the summer term. The educational quality of the nursery has been judged as satisfactory, so the nursery can take part in the scheme. Jodi's parents pay £85 a week, for her full-time place. For three terms, while Jodi is 4, they can use the vouchers to help with some of the cost of the nursery place.

Aylea is 3 and has a place at the nursery class at her local primary school. She goes five mornings a week, and has almost finished her first term. Her mum does not have to pay anything for her place. Next term, Aylea will be 4, and her mum will soon receive a voucher application form. For Aylea to continue in the nursery class, her mum must give the school the vouchers. The value of the vouchers only goes some way towards paying for the nursery place – the local education authority pays the difference.

At the time of writing, the first phase of the scheme was just about to start. It's difficult to predict how it will work. The situation may change if and when the second phase of the scheme starts in April 1997. You can contact the Department of Education and Employment or their helpline for further information (see 'Useful organizations').

It is a fact that there are not enough nursery class places for all the 4-year-olds whose parents want nursery education. The government believes that the voucher scheme will help to create more places. The idea is that as more parents will be able to afford places, so more places will be created – in other words, supply will increase to meet the demand. That may or may not happen.

The other important fact to remember is that the value of the vouchers do not pay the full cost of preschool provision. Parents on low wages who can't pay the difference between the full cost of care and the value of the vouchers will still not be able to afford a childcare place for their 4-year-old in private sector provision.

2
What do people need from childcare?

When you are choosing a nursery, playgroup or childminder, you need to weigh up your needs, your child's needs and – odd though it may sound – the needs of the person providing care for your child. All of these can change over time. As your child grows up and your family or work situation changes, you will need to check every so often to make sure that your childcare arrangements are still meeting everyone's needs.

What children need

Children are all different. Because of these differences, children's needs vary. What a child needs from childcare will depend on their age and their stage of development. When you are thinking about childcare for a young baby, don't forget that your baby will soon be a toddler, and then a preschooler. Try to look at each childcare setting from the point of view of different age groups. For example, you may find a place that provides wonderful care for babies but doesn't have a good range of play materials for older children. What do you do? You could choose to send your child there until they were older, and then move them somewhere else. However, it is best to keep change to a minimum, as young children often find it upsetting.

Of course, you could choose to have a variety of childcare arrangements. For example, you may want to start using a childminder when your child is a few months old. The childminder could take your child to a toddler group at 15 months old, and then to a nursery class or playgroup at 3 or 4 years old. This could be one way of meeting the changing needs of a growing child while keeping disruption to a minimum.

As children develop, so their needs change. Children develop very quickly between birth and school age. To keep a track of these rapid changes, experts split child development into different areas (see Box 2.1).

Information box 2.1: Important areas of child development

- Communication and language (talking and understanding)
- Thinking and problem-solving (counting, doing puzzles)
- Physical (standing, walking, running)
- Social and emotional (making friends, showing feelings)
- Self-help (dressing, feeding)

Every parent wants to know whether their child is developing normally. Answering this question can be very difficult. Perfectly normal children develop at very different rates. Your 2-year-old could be a chatterbox, while the 2-year-old next door might only say one or two words. Within a year, there could be almost no difference between them.

Children don't develop in a smooth, even way. For example, they may be better than average when it comes to talking, but be a bit slower when it comes to physical growth. Most children reach what the experts call their 'developmental milestones' eventually. Still, it is very important to remember that experience plays a vital part. Practice makes perfect – for example, a child spoken to regularly by adults is more likely to develop good language skills. Choosing childcare is all about giving children the experiences they need to develop their full potential.

What a child needs from childcare will change as the child gets older and learns new skills. Remember, age is only a rough guide to development. Box 2.2 gives some examples of how to link what a child can do with what they need from their surroundings.

Information box 2.2: What a child can do, and what a child needs from childcare

	What a child can do	What a child needs from their surroundings
Up to about 6 months old	Roll over, kick, wave arms and legs about	A soft, clean and safe surface where they can spend time on their front and back, kicking freely
	See clearly, reach and hold things, put them in its mouth	Plenty to look at, especially people; mobiles in cots, soft toys and easily-held objects like rattles.
	Make noises, squeal and scream	Lots of talking to (face to face), and games like 'peep-bo'

Up to about 1 year old	Crawl	Safe play area where fragile/ dangerous objects can't be reached
	Hold a cup, feed self with spoon	Chance to practice feeding themselves, no matter how messily
	Babble, recognize own name, understand but not speak	A lot of talking to, especially using own name; simple nursery rhymes and games like 'This little piggy'
Up to about 18 months old	Turn pages of a book and point to pictures	To be read short, repetitive stories and be given plenty of picture books
	Play with simple toys	Bricks, cars, balls, dolls, big boxes, things to push or pull
	Use crayons to make marks on paper	Paper and large crayons; supervision to make sure child draws on paper and not other things!
Up to about 2 years old	Run, play independently	Daily exercise in a safe outdoor space like a playground or park
	Good control of hands	Plenty of toys like building bricks, simple wooden jigsaws and things to sort and stack
	Use up to 200 words	A lot of talking to, including explanations of rules; plenty of story-telling
Up to about 3 years old	Carry cups of liquid, use a paint brush and scissors	Toys for construction, regular chances to do cutting, sticking, painting and drawing

	Wash own hands, dress self	Chance to practice washing and dressing without being rushed
	Play pretend games, share toys	Adults to join in make-believe play; other children to play with
Up to about 4 years old	Use stairs, throw and kick a ball, hop, skip and jump	Regular chance to play with other children in open spaces, with bats, balls and climbing equipment
	Draw recognizable objects, write some letters, concentrate on a task for up to 20 minutes	Plenty of drawing and writing materials; more difficult construction toys like Lego; chance to get away from younger children
	Understand 'why' and 'how' explanations, make up stories	To be talked to in a more adult way; more complicated stories to read, fewer pictures; someone to listen to and encourage stories

Some children have special needs – physical, educational or emotional. Many people argue that *all* children have special needs. Catering for these needs can sometimes demand more time or different kinds of care. Development for these children may take a different course.

Keeping an eye on a child's development is obviously very important. The sooner we spot potential problems, the easier it is to offer the right kind of help. Nevertheless, comparing a child's development with another child, or with some fixed idea of what is 'normal', can be a mistake. It's much better to make regular checks, and then compare what a child could do some months ago with what they can do now. This is the best way of recognizing any hiccups in development, and avoids making comparisons with other children. Children are all different, and it is important that we recognize these differences, instead of worrying about whether a child is 'normal'. Anyway, how would you describe a 'normal' child?

Thinking about your child's temperament can be a good idea when it comes to making childcare arrangements. Children, like adults, vary in the way they react to different situations. They have different temperaments or characters. Some children are outgoing and chat happily to everyone they meet. Others are shy and say very little until they know people well. The same can be true of babies: some are fussy and take a long time to settle, while others are more easygoing. Two children can react very differently to the same situation. Box 2.3 sets out some questions to ask yourself in deciding what form of childcare would best suit your child. In the end, only you can answer these questions. No one knows your child better than you do.

Information box 2.3: Choosing care to suit your child. Ask yourself these questions:

- Would my child be happier being the youngest or eldest child in a group?
- Would a home setting be better than a nursery setting?
- Would they do better in a large group of children, or with only one or two?
- Would they get more out of an informal atmosphere, or do they need a more structured environment?

What parents need

You may be thinking of using childcare because you are planning to return to work. Maybe you want some time for yourself, or perhaps you think that spending time with other children will be good for your child. Part of choosing the right type of childcare involves thinking about your needs too. You need good quality childcare that is dependable, and will continue to be right for your child as they grow up. Your own needs and circumstances will be a big influence on the childcare arrangement you make – Box 2.4 gives some examples.

Information box 2.4: What a parent has, and what a parent needs from childcare

What a parent has	What a parent needs from childcare
Worries about leaving their child with a carer	Sympathetic attitude; invitation to stay with child for first few visits; willingness to answer queries
A full-time job	Full-time care with hours to suit
Irregular working hours or shifts	Carers to be flexible in terms of time when children can be dropped off and collected
Extreme work or family demands	Some help and advice with parenting; short breaks from responsibilities of childcare
A child with special needs	Carers who can work with parents and other professionals
Desire to know how their child is developing	Careful and regular record-keeping of child's progress
Concerns about their child	A time and a place to talk to carers

---

What childcare providers need

Professionals who provide childcare – usually women – have needs too. We sometimes forget about the needs of carers, arguing that since we are paying them to care for our children, their needs are not our concern.

As every parent knows, caring for children day in and day out is hard work. Providing childcare is an important and valuable job. Carers have responsibility for the health and safety of the children in their care, and play a vital role in encouraging children's development. We should give professional childcarers the credit and reward such an important job deserves.

It's a sad fact that the people who provide care for our children often do not receive the rewards they deserve. Many professional childcarers have to put up with poor working conditions and low pay. Parents should be worried about this state of affairs – research has shown that where childcare workers have better working conditions, the quality of care provided is better – Box 2.5 gives some examples.

Information box 2.5: What a childcarer does, and what a childcarer needs

What a childcarer does	What a childcarer needs
Looks after children all day, every day	Short but regular breaks away from the children in a quiet place; for childminders, time to unwind at the end of the day
Organizes a variety of appropriate activities	Time within the working day to plan ahead
A difficult, demanding and important job	Good working conditions that include paid holidays and sick leave
Keeps track of children's progress	Time during the working day to keep proper records
Promotes child development	Chance to keep up with new ideas and methods through further training
Takes responsibility for children	Recognition from parents of a job well done
Has a home and family of their own	Parents who collect their children at agreed times

3
How do you decide what's best for your child?

What to choose

Which type of childcare is best? There is no simple answer. It depends on what you want for your child. If you want your child looked after in a quiet, friendly, family atmosphere, then perhaps a childminder might be best. If you want your child to get used to the hustle and bustle of being with lots of other children, then maybe a nursery is the answer. What suits you may not suit someone else. What is right for your child now might not be appropriate in two years' time. You could decide on a mixture – for example, your child could spend part of the day at playgroup and the rest of the day with a childminder.

Whatever type of care you choose, it is *quality* of care that is most important. Children don't learn new things automatically. They need the right kind of stimulation and encouragement. Good quality childcare gives your child the chance to develop to the best of their abilities. Even at this young age, experiences in childcare can have an effect on how a child grows up. Successful development is more likely to happen when children receive good quality childcare – not just educational development but emotional and social development too. What is more, children who receive good quality childcare are often happier than children subjected to poor quality care. Quality must be at the top of your shopping list for childcare. An important aim of this book is to tell you more about quality and how to recognize it. We will return to the question of quality in the chapters that follow.

The practical considerations set out in Box 3.1 will often limit

---

Information box 3.1: Considerations that will affect your choice of childcare

Convenience   How easy is it to get to? Is it near home, or work? Is it on the way to work for me or my partner?

Cost   How much will it cost? Can I afford it?

Hours   How many hours a day do I need someone to look after my child? How flexible are my employers?

Availability   What is on offer in my area?

your choices. Still, once you are clear about your basic requirements, you can begin to look at what is best for you and your child. But how can you clarify your basic requirements?

We all have dreams about what we would like, given unlimited choice – the ideal job, the ideal house. Being content with what we can actually have rather than what we dream of having is sometimes difficult. The same is true when it comes to childcare. You could be very lucky and find exactly what you are looking for. That's great. But for most of us, the reality is that we are not going to find exactly what we want – for example, you may decide that a workplace nursery is the answer for you and your child, but find that employers in your area don't run workplace nurseries.

Finding childcare is often a matter of compromise. You will probably have to accept that you can't get *everything* you want. The trick is to think of the things that are most important when it comes to a childcare place, then make the choice that achieves as many of these as possible. Listing the things you want from childcare and putting them in some sort of order – most important to least important – is one way to start. You may be willing to do without some things, while there may be others you consider essential.

Take the example of Jane, who is looking for childcare for her 3-year-old daughter, Sophie, because she wants to go back to her job as a sales manager. Jane has worked out that to make it worth her going back to work financially, she can spend no more than £70 a week on childcare. She wants her daughter to receive some formal teaching so that she doesn't feel out of her depth when she starts school. Because Sophie can be a bit shy, Jane would like her to be in a small group of other children. Jane works on flexitime, so she can adapt her hours to suit whatever the childcare arrangements may offer, but on some days she has to run very important conferences for other sales managers, which means there are some days at work she just can't miss. On these conference days, she may have to work a little later than usual. In emergencies, Jane's mum, who also works full-time, could collect Sophie from the nursery, but because Jane's mum doesn't have a car, Sophie would need to be somewhere not too far away. Box 3.2 shows Jane's list of priorities for her childcare choices.

Making a list encourages you to think about what you would like. When making any choice, it is important to make a careful and informed choice – this means being armed with all the facts.

Information box 3.2: Making a list of priorities

Features	Priority
Less than £70 a week	A
No more than ten minutes from home	A
Well-qualified staff	A
Emphasis on education	A
No possibility of last-minute let-downs	A
Within five minutes from work	B
Small groups of children	B
Flexibility over pick-up times	B
Family atmosphere	C
Open from 8.30 a.m.	C

4
Good quality childcare and the law

How can we define good quality childcare?

This is a difficult question to answer – it's a bit like asking someone to define beauty. As we all know, beauty is in the eye of the beholder. The same is true of quality – it means different things to different people.

Parents, childcare professionals, psychologists, politicians, local authority under-eights advisers and children all have different opinions about childcare, resulting from their differing points of view. That is not to say that they wouldn't agree on lots of things – for example, everyone would agree that children need to be in safe surroundings. Nobody would want a child playing in the same room as an unguarded electric fire. It's not so easy to get agreement about less clear-cut topics. Take children's use of creative play materials, for example. Childcare experts often say that being able to help themselves to things is important for children, as it means that children learn about choice and how to use some materials with others. On the other hand, some professional nursery workers prefer to limit the variety of materials children have access to. They say that children just get confused by having too much to choose from, and letting children help themselves just makes a mess that staff have to clear up.

When parents go into a nursery or a childminder's home for the first time, their attention is usually drawn to the way adults and children respond to each other. In any childcare setting, it is very important that children and adults get on. Talk to parents about quality childcare, and eventually you will hear them say '... as long as the children look happy'. Unfortunately, there's more to it than that. Children can be very happy playing with a wonderfully caring adult in a room that has scalding hot central heating radiators or uncovered electric sockets. Putting children's safety at risk is not part of good quality care, however happy the children might look.

As you can see, getting everyone to agree on what makes good quality childcare is always going to be difficult. That's another reason why it's so important that you think carefully about what *you* want for your child. Once you've made your mind up about what quality means for you, you can start looking around your area for what's on offer.

What does the law say about good quality childcare?

As you start to find out more about childcare, inevitably you will hear people talking about the Children Act. The 1989 Children Act passed into law in 1991. It sets out rules and regulations to do with children's welfare, and gives local authorities legal powers and responsibilities for making sure that people providing services for children obey these rules and regulations. Like most legal documents, the Children Act is both long and complicated. The Department of Health has produced booklets (called Guidance and Regulations) to help local authorities apply the Act.

Part of the Children Act sets out rules and regulations to do with childcare. The most important rule concerns registration. *The local authority must register anyone who is paid for looking after children under the age of 8 for more than two hours a day. Anyone who is being paid without being registered is breaking the law.* Payment doesn't have to be in money: the law also covers payment in kind – that is, the return of some favour or service. The only people who do not have to register are relatives of the child, nannies (caring for children from no more than two families in their home), babysitters and au pairs.

What do people have to do to be registered?

Any person who wants to be a childminder or open a nursery or playgroup must apply to their local authority for registration. The local authority must carry out a series of checks before they register anybody to provide childcare. Boxes 4.1–4.4 tell you about the matters the Children Act says local authorities have to check. These checks include:

1 checks on the person
2 checks on buildings
3 checks on equipment

As well as checking on the person applying for registration, the local authority also checks out other people who live or work with the applicant – these usually include a childminder's partner, or, in a nursery or playgroup, other care workers. They make the checks with the police, health authority and social services. This is to make sure that these people do not have a known involvement in child abuse cases or other criminal activities, or do not have health problems which would make them unsuitable to be around young children.

Information box 4.1: Local authority registration checks on the person

- Previous experience of looking after or working with young children
- Qualification and/or training in a relevant field
- The ability to provide warm and consistent care
- Knowledge and understanding of multicultural issues and people of various racial origins
- A commitment and sufficient knowledge to treat all children as individuals and with equal concern
- Physical health
- Mental stability, integrity and flexibility
- No known involvement in criminal cases involving abuse of children

---

Information box 4.2: Local authority registration checks on buildings

- Safety of outside play areas (for example, fencing of ponds, no access to roads)
- Safety of fires, electrical sockets, windows, floor coverings and glass doors
- Safety in the kitchen or cooking area
- Use of stairgates
- Presence of pets, and arrangements for their control
- Arrangements for keeping the premises clean
- Provision for rest and sleep
- Washing and toilet facilities, and hygiene
- Fire safety (for example, smoke detectors, matches locked away)

Information box 4.3: Local authority registration checks on equipment

- Appropriate toys for the ages and stages of the children
- Equipment and furniture should conform to a British Standard, where one exists
- Amount of equipment and furniture and their quality and types should be adequate for the number of children and adults in the setting
- Organization of kitchen equipment in nurseries and play-groups must follow environmental health regulations

Information box 4.4: Additional local authority registration checks on playgroups and day nurseries

- Sufficient space for each age group
- No more than 26 children in one room
- Separate areas for quiet, noisy and messy activities
- One toilet and handbasin for every ten children
- Separate toilet facilities for staff
- Office space and staff room
- Access to outside play space

Additional checks if infants and toddlers are taken:

- Each baby to be looked after by the same person during each shift
- Staff to have knowledge of child development in the very young
- Separate room for babies and toddlers

Having read about all these matters that local authorities check, we could forgive parents for thinking that they don't need to worry about quality. Apparently, any nursery or childminder who is registered must be doing a good job. But – and it is a very big but – there is a catch. The law, as it's laid out in the Children Act, says that local authorities must only *consider* the results of these checks – local authorities can still register a provider, even if that provider doesn't pass all the checks listed. The law states that they must treat each application for registration on its individual merits. In practice, local authorities have the right to choose which items from the list of checks they want to apply and to add items of their own should they wish.

Providers need comply with only five conditions to be registered. These govern:

1   numbers of children
2   numbers of staff
3   maintenance and safety of the premises and equipment
4   keeping records of staff/household members, family details of children, etc
5   notification of changes with respect to people working or living in the premises

Local authorities must make sure that all registered persons meet these five requirements.

Registration entails only a very few compulsory checks, but we have known of some dishonest providers who have even tried to get around these – for example, requirements for staff numbers have been met by bringing in temporary people on the day when the local authority carries out its registration check. Because registration is no guarantee of good quality care, it is important that parents know what to look for. As paying customers, you have the right to demand that providers offer good quality childcare.

How do you know if the person is registered?

Once the local authority registers a provider, it gives them a certificate of registration. Always check whether a childminder, nursery, or playgroup is registered by asking to see their registration certificate. The local authority also keeps a list of all registered childminders, playgroups and nurseries. If you do find an unregistered person who you think would be good at looking after your child, get them to register first.

The Children Act says that local authorities must inspect each registered provider – whether a childminder, nursery or playgroup – at least once a year, to make sure that standards are maintained. In all cases, inspection visits are pre-arranged with the provider. During the inspection visit, an inspector will check that the provider is meeting the requirements. Some local authorities are able to make additional, unannounced visits, but many simply don't have the resources to carry out more than one annual inspection.

Does registration guarantee good quality care?

Registration does not necessarily prove that a provider offers good quality care. It only guarantees that the standard of care is acceptable. The system of registration, inspection visits and training enables local authorities to help providers maintain and, sometimes, improve standards, but it is no guarantee of quality. That's why it's important for parents to check the quality of care for themselves.

Registration and insurance

One final point about using a registered childcare provider: *registered providers must accept legal responsibility for the children in their care.* Parents can sue them for damages if an accident or injury involving a child occurs. Consequently, registered providers take out an insurance policy which covers them in this situation. Always ask to see insurance certificates. Unregistered childcare providers will have no insurance. If anything happened to your child while being looked after by an unregistered person, you could have serious problems getting financial compensation. If an accident resulted in expensive medical bills or meant you having to give up work altogether, you and your whole family could suffer.

Using unregistered carers is unfair to those who go to the trouble and expense of obeying the law. People who don't register sometimes charge less, which keeps the wages of all professional childcarers lower than they should be. Using unregistered carers is also selfish. Registration helps to improve standards of care – if you encourage some people not to register, standards of care for all children suffer.

Part two

In Chapter 4, we mentioned Guidance and Regulations booklets produced by the Department of Health to help local authorities apply the Children Act. Advice provided in the Guidance and Regulations is written with the help of childcare experts. The booklet about childcare (DoH, 1991) includes a list of 13 factors that affect quality:

1 adult–child interactions
2 interactions between children
3 recognizing children's developmental needs
4 type of contract/involvement between parent and provider
5 number of staff and size of group
6 continuity, training and experience of staff
7 equal opportunities policies in employment and service delivery
8 ability to structure and support children's learning
9 elements in programme of activities
10 children's involvement in planning activities

11   elements of imagination, challenge and adventure in activities

12   organization, display and accessibility of equipment, toys and materials

13   attention to health, safety and type of physical environment

In part two of *Choosing Childcare*, we look at each of these 13 aspects that affect quality. For each, we explain what it means, why it is important, and how it might appear in practice. Because of the obvious differences between childminders and nurseries, some aspects of quality differ in detail in each setting. Where this is the case, we have made it clear. We have not covered sessional care here, by which we mean playgroups or nursery classes. However, many considerations that affect quality apply across all types of setting.

Part two examines the 13 things to look for in good quality childcare in four chapters:

- Chapter 5 – Relationships in good quality childcare
- Chapter 6 – Group size, training and equal opportunities
- Chapter 7 – Activities in childcare settings
- Chapter 8 – The physical environment

5
Relationships in good quality childcare

Adult–child interactions

Why are adult–child interactions important to quality?

Adult–child interactions are to do with how adults relate to children. They include what adults say to children, how they say it (tone of voice), and how they appear when they're talking to children (facial expression).

The tone of voice an adult uses when talking to a child is very important. It gives a message to the child about what the adult is thinking. Even infants as young as 6 months, who can't talk, can tell the difference between different tones of voice. Harsh, angry tones often make children feel quite scared. Children who are frightened are much less likely to learn new things. They simply won't take a risk of getting something wrong if they think an adult might criticize, mock or shout at them.

As children grow, so their ability to let adults know what they are thinking and feeling develops. Babies can only cry, squeal, smile or wave their arms and legs about. By the time they are 5, most children can talk, understand instructions and make out from tone of voice when someone is angry, sad or happy. Learning a language in five years is quite an achievement, especially when you think about all the other things children have to learn. Children don't just learn about language automatically – they learn by watching, listening and talking to the people around them. That's why it is so important that adults provide good quality interaction for young children: without it, children will find it more difficult to develop the language skills they need.

Facial expressions, especially eye contact, are an important part of adult–child interactions. Picking children up, crouching down or sitting on the floor or at a table with them can encourage talking. Arranging furniture so that adults can sit at the same level as children helps as well. Being physically close also makes it easier to be warm and affectionate and maintain eye-contact. Seeing adults down on the floor or sitting at tables with children is a good sign.

It's also important to see how quickly adults react to what children do or say. When adults are sensitive and responsive to their needs, children tend to be happier, feel safer, and find it easier to learn new things.

What to look for

Parents often say that the atmosphere in a nursery or at a childminder's home is a big influence on their choice of childcare. Atmosphere is a good indicator of the quality of adult–child interactions. In a relaxed and friendly atmosphere, children smile, laugh, talk to adults and to each other, and ask adults for help. Adults will talk calmly rather than shout, will use a warm, friendly tone of voice, and won't threaten or criticize children. Boxes 5.1

and 5.2 give examples of desirable and undesirable behaviour on the part of caregivers.

Information box 5.1: Desirable behaviour in carers

You *do* want to see adults:

- answering children's questions
- asking children open questions (those beginning with 'what', 'why', 'who' or 'how')
- listening to what children say
- looking at children when they are talking to them
- showing interest in what children are doing
- encouraging children by praising them
- using a warm and friendly tone of voice
- being aware of children's moods (like cuddling a child who is miserable)
- giving children tasks that they can do
- showing affection, warmth and respect in their physical contact with children
- reacting quickly and appropriately (like picking up an infant who is crying)

Communication is particularly important for children who haven't yet started to talk. Very young children need lots of physical contact. Infants are learning even during routine activities like feeding, nappy-changing and cuddling. Even young children can work out whether someone likes them and enjoys being with them. There are several things to look for. Adults should hold infants while they are bottle fed. You do not want to see small children lying in cots or baby chairs with a bottle being held in their mouths. A good care worker will always pick an infant up and soothe them when they are upset. Adults talking and playing with infants during nappy-changing is another good sign.

Information box 5.2: Undesirable behaviour in carers

You *do not* want to see adults:

- ignoring children when they are talking, crying or looking lost
- not joining in activities or giving help when it's needed
- using a harsh, cold tone of voice
- talking only to keep order (like 'Don't do that' or 'Go and play over there')
- looking bored
- talking to each other more than to children
- being unaffectionate (children rarely picked up, held or cuddled)
- leaving children for long periods without adult contact (infants left awake in a cot or high chair)

Communication like this helps infants to feel safe and secure. When infants feel safe and secure, they feel more confident about exploring their surroundings. More exploring means more learning.

Interactions between children

Why are interactions between children important to quality?

Playing together helps children learn about sharing, about settling arguments and about getting on with each other – these are what psychologists call 'social skills'. Social skills are vital when it comes to making and keeping friends. The more children mix with other children, the more opportunity they have to develop their social skills. Children used to playing with other children are often more outgoing, and can play together for longer without getting bored or falling out with the others.

Nursery workers and childminders should try to create situations that encourage interactions between children. They can do this by getting children to play in small groups. Take an activity like painting or art work, for example – children will benefit most when paints and other materials are set out on different tables, with three or four chairs at each table. These kinds of situations encourage children to talk and co-operate with each other – for example, they may have to decide who uses the yellow paint first, or work out that they can't all use the glue at the same time. It's a question of organizing different activities for small groups of children, not having all the children together in one big group for the same activity. Good nurseries divide rooms into activity areas which encourage children to play in small groups.

Adults can help children play together. Children should be encouraged to talk to each other, rewarded for unselfish behaviour, and sometimes just left alone to work things out for themselves. Boxes 5.3 and 5.4 give examples of desirable and undesirable behaviour on the part of children.

Information box 5.3: Desirable behaviour in children

You *do* want to see children:

- talking to each other regularly
- playing in small groups
- sharing toys or other equipment without squabbling
- being given things to do that encourage co-operation
- helping each other
- being praised for sharing or being kind

Information box 5.4: Undesirable behaviour in children

You *do not* want to see children:

- constantly fighting over toys or equipment
- playing or working in large groups all the time
- being told to keep quiet every five minutes
- looking left out
- bullying each other
- talking only to adults

It's easy to provide opportunities for children to play with each other in a nursery, but for childminders, it is more difficult. Yet children looked after by childminders can still have the chance to play with their peers. Depending on the ages of the children, childminders can use a parent/toddler group, playgroup or nursery for at least part of the day. In some areas, childminders also have groups where they meet up with other childminders and the children in their care. Ask about these kinds of activities when you're choosing your childminder.

Recognizing children's developmental needs

Why is recognizing children's developmental needs important to quality?

Successful development is all about children learning new things. Good quality childcare provides the kind of activities and equipment that help children's development. During these early years, it's important that children enjoy learning. The more they enjoy learning, the more they will want to learn new things. Give children toys they find difficult to play with, or ask them to do things needing skills they don't yet have, and they will get bored and frustrated. Nobody likes to fail. Succeeding is just as enjoyable for children as it is for adults. To make sure that children do things they will enjoy, adults need a good understanding of their developmental needs. That means knowing something about child development in general, and keeping a careful note of how well each particular child is doing.

Adults need to know what children can and can't do at different ages and stages. Getting it wrong can be very easy. A good carer will know which activities and materials help children develop. The trick is to avoid asking children to do things they find boring or frustrating
– for example, there's not much point giving a toddler a game involving threading string through small holes. As any good carer would know, toddlers haven't learnt the necessary manual skills. The answer would be to give a child of this age cotton reels or other objects with large holes. That way, they can succeed. Another good example of adapting to developmental needs might

be providing sponges for painting if a child is unable to hold a paintbrush.

Because development unfolds at different rates, children of the same age don't all behave in the same way. One child may spend all morning making a picture, while another may have finished in a few minutes. Some need time to learn new skills. Others grasp ideas quite quickly. Putting pressure on a child to finish an activity before they are ready can easily make them anxious. Anxious children don't learn well. On the other hand, children who have to sit and wait for others to finish get bored and frustrated. It doesn't take long for boredom and frustration to lead to misbehaviour. Balancing the needs of all children in a group is not easy. Without a good understanding of each child's needs and abilities, it is almost impossible.

Meeting children's individual needs means keeping a close watch on their development. Regular observation and assessment of children are very important. As well as keeping track of development, regular assessment also helps identify any physical problems a child may have, like hearing loss or speech problems. The sooner problems of this sort are spotted, the more likely it is that permanent damage can be prevented. Of course, assessment of young children in childcare settings needs to be done properly but sensitively. The kind of methods used to assess adults are often inappropriate.

The law doesn't say that care providers have to keep records of developmental information about individual children. However, a government report on the educational experiences of young children said that keeping these kinds of records is good practice. According to the report, the main purpose of keeping records should be to ensure that educational provision is properly planned and evaluated. Developmental information should be used:

● to plan work in a way that takes account of a child's abilities

- to identify children who may need special help
- to provide information for parents and others involved in the child's future education
- to evaluate the quality of care being provided

It is not just childcare providers who can keep records of a child's progress – parents can make a valuable contribution too. After all, parents know their child best. Keeping records on developmental progress gives parents and care workers a chance to work together in planning and evaluating a child's education.

Good quality care will include regular observation and recording of children's progress. There's no strict rule about how often information should be collected. The more often children are assessed, the more detailed the records will be. Perhaps more important is that observation and recording is done regularly. It can be once a month or once every three months – regularity is the key. Failing to carry out regular assessments can lead to developmental delays being missed.

Collecting information is one thing, using it properly is another matter. It makes no sense to monitor a child's progress and then not tell parents or other carers what has been found. Guidelines on good practice usually recommend keeping open records – that means you can see your child's developmental record on request. A formal meeting to discuss progress is usually best. Staff meetings, child reviews with parents, and open days/evenings are good examples of formal situations. Informal discussions with care staff at the beginning and end of the day are useful, but should not replace formal meetings.

Some people think that keeping developmental records is not really the job of a childminder. The National Childminding Association does not agree. They recommend that childminders should keep records, including observations of children's behaviour and development. The information they collect can then be discussed with parents.

Box 5.5 gives a checklist of points to bear in mind in gauging whether the care provider is monitoring and catering for children's developmental needs.

Information box 5.5: Recognizing children's developmental needs

Check that:

- children of different ages are given different things to do
- children don't seem bored or frustrated
- adults don't pressurize children to finish activities quickly
- regular assessments of children's abilities are made
- proper developmental records are kept on every child
- progress of each child is discussed at formal staff meetings
- parents have an opportunity for formal discussions with staff

---

Type of contract/involvement between parent and provider

Why is the type of contract/involvement between parent and provider important to quality?

The Guidance and Regulations to the Children Act say that childcare providers should recognize and respect the role of parents in their children's upbringing. Experts have written a lot about parental involvement in recent years – the phrase they often use is 'partnership with parents'. A good relationship between parent and provider is important. We have already explained why parents and carers need to exchange information about development. Having parents and care providers working together is obviously in the best interests of the child. Good quality childcare depends on it.

Good relationships are built on good communication. Your child lives in two worlds: the world of home and the world of childcare. What happens to them in one setting will affect their behaviour in the other. Care providers need to know what the child has been doing at home, just as parents need to know what has been happening while the child is with the provider.

Good communication can be formal, informal, or a mixture of both. Informal chats at the beginning and end of the day between parents and providers are, hopefully, very common. Keeping a diary is another way of sharing information – a small notebook or exercise book will do. Both parents and providers can use it to keep brief notes about what children have been doing during the day, evening or weekend. The diary can be passed between home and the child-carer on a daily or weekly basis. Diaries help if finding time to talk at the beginning or end of the day is difficult for either parent or carer. More formal ways of communicating, particularly in nurseries, are notice boards, parent mail boxes and regular newsletters. Parent evenings and open days are also very useful.

Nurseries that have a written policy about parental involvement have obviously put some thought into the issue. They may ask that parents get involved in activities such as:

● parent meetings
● parent advisory/nursery management committees
● fundraising, publicity, socials

- training and discussion groups

Not all parents will want to get involved in everything. Pressures on time and money may limit the extent to which some parents can contribute.

Most local authorities and professional organizations concerned with childcare strongly recommend having a written contract. That applies to nurseries as well as childminders. Chapters 9 and 10 deal with childcare contracts in more detail.

Finally, it makes sense to have some idea of the aims, objectives and policies of the childcare provider, to give you some idea on what things you agree. Ideally, this information should be in writing – for example, a prospectus or brochure about the nursery. It's easy to forget the details of information given during a visit to the provider.

Box 5.6 gives a checklist of points to consider in assessing parent–provider relationships.

Information box 5.6: Parent/provider relationships

Check that:

- there are regular parent/staff meetings
- providers have time to chat to parents
- the nursery has a room in which parents can talk to staff
- there is a written contract (this applies to nurseries and childminders)
- there is a noticeboard and/or newsletter
- there is written information about care provision
- parents are encouraged to drop in any time

6
Group size, training and equal opportunities

Number of staff and size of group

Why are numbers of staff important to quality?

In nurseries or other childcare situations, we commonly call the number of children per adult the 'adult–child ratio'. The adult–child ratio when two adults are looking after a group of ten children is 1:5. Adult–child ratios affect the behaviour of both adults and children – this is especially true when it comes to infants and toddlers. Having fewer children for each adult to look after means that adults have more time to spend with each child. Having more time means that adults can be more responsive, more sensitive to children's needs and more involved with the children in their care. The more children an adult has to look after, the less time they can devote to each individual child.

Good adult–child ratios lead to less distress and upset among children, because adults are more able to spot trouble before it gets out of hand. For the same reason, potentially dangerous situations are less likely to end in disaster. Infants will be more active in nurseries where adults have enough time to spend with them. Good adult–child ratios will often mean that adults don't have to spend so much time shouting at children and ordering them about. Adults will have more opportunity to do desirable things, like talking to children, showing affection and taking an interest in what children are doing.

As you may have guessed, good adult–child ratios are not only good for children, they also make the job of caring much more enjoyable for adults. Being able to work with a few children is much more rewarding than having to worry about controlling a large group. The more children an adult has to look after, the more the job is about control and the less about quality interaction.

The Children Act makes *recommendations* about adult–child ratios, but the recommended ratios vary depending on the age of children. Infants and toddlers need much more physical care than older children – for example, infants need to be fed and to have their nappies changed. The recommended adult–child ratio for younger children is higher to take account of these different needs. The adult–child ratios given in Boxes 6.1 and 6.2 for nurseries and childminders are the *minimum* acceptable level.

In some nurseries, adults whom they include in their adult–child ratios for the purposes of complying with the Children Act don't actually spend time with the children – they may be doing other things, like organizing timetables or supervising kitchen staff. Look out for this when you are visiting nurseries. Nurseries should always maintain adult–child ratios. Adults don't have to be constantly talking or playing with children, but they should be in the same room, listening and keeping an eye on things.

It may be worth noting that adult–child ratios for 4-year-olds in nursery classes and reception classes are a little different to those

Information box 6.1: Adult–child ratios in day nurseries and playgroups, as recommended by the Children Act

Age range	Recommended adult–child ratio
0–2 years	1 adult to 3 children
2–3 years	1 adult to 4 children
3–5 years	1 adult to 8 children

Ratios should be *higher* than recommended in nurseries where some care staff are not fully qualified, or where very young babies are cared for.

Information box 6.2: Adult–child ratios for childminders, as recommended by the Children Act

Age range	Recommended number of children per childminder
0–5 years	Maximum of 3, of whom only 1 can be under 1 year old
0–8 years	No more than 6, of whom only 3 can be under 5
5–8 years	No more than 6
Over 8 years	No recommendations

Ratios must include a childminder's own children.

that apply in day nurseries. In nursery classes, the recommended ratio for 4-year-olds is 1:13, and in reception classes it is 1:13 or 1:15 if an assistant is working with a teacher, and 1:26 or 1:30 where a teacher has no assistant. On the face of it, these ratios look much worse than the 1:8 recommended for day nurseries. However, remember that nursery and reception classes always have *trained* staff. Teachers generally have four years of training, compared with an average of two years for nursery nurses. Also, children tend to spend less time in nursery or reception classes.

Why is size of group important to quality?

Group size is really only relevant to playgroups and nurseries. Remember: *the law does not allow childminders to look after more than six children under the age of 8, including their own.* Group size has important effects on both child development and nursery staff. Small groups allow children to get to know each other well. Children looked after in small groups are often more friendly, more talkative and happier about joining in with other children.

For nursery staff, coping with large groups often means spending less quality time with children, and more time organizing and controlling them. As you will see when you visit different nurseries, larger groups often mean more noise and more problems to sort out between children, and so more stress for adults.

The Children Act says that in nurseries with more than 50 places, they should look after children in groups of no more than 26. Even in nurseries with less than 50 places, groups of more than 26 children are probably not a good idea.

The younger children are, the smaller the group should be. The Guidance and Regulations to the Children Act recommend groups of no more than six to eight for children aged 3–4 years old.

Nurseries have different ways of organizing children into groups. A common approach has been a 'family group' system –

children of different ages are put into the same group, cared for by one or two nursery staff. The idea is to re-create ordinary family life. This system also gives nursery workers a bit more variety. More recently, experts have suggested that putting children of similar ages in the same groups may be better.

There are several advantages to having groups of same-aged children:

- Working with a group at similar stages of development is easier for nursery staff.
- Nursery staff don't have to worry about older children getting bored or frustrated.
- Children receive more attention because they are all doing similar things.

Having groups of children of about the same age also helps a nursery when it comes to organizing room space and activities. Creating areas that stimulate children to the maximum of their potential is much easier when you are catering for a particular age group.

Continuity, training and experience of staff

Why is continuity of care important for quality?

Many of us don't like change. Moving home, starting a new job or even having children are events we find stressful. Change is disruptive – it often puts us out of sorts. Continuity of care is particularly important for children. Being looked after by one different person after another can cause delays in the development of language, as well as emotional and behavioural difficulties. Providing stability and keeping change to a minimum is part of good quality childcare.

When a child has only a few carers, children and adults can get to know and understand each other. Children have their own little habits and peculiarities, just as most adults do. When children and adults know each other well, they stand a better chance of understanding each other's behaviour. For example, a parent can make sense of their toddler's speech, although someone else might not have a clue what they are saying.

Regular changes in nursery staff can cause unwanted change and instability for children. High staff turnover can occur for many different reasons. One common reason for staff leaving after only a short time in the job is to do with pay and working conditions. When people are happy with pay and conditions, they are less likely to leave. When you visit nurseries, it's worth asking about the numbers of new staff, or the number of people who have left in the last year. Staff leaving a nursery, particularly if they have been there for only a short time, may be a warning that something is not quite right.

The pay and conditions for carers can affect your child. As employees, we are all too aware that good working conditions generally make us happier at work – for example, there has been much talk recently about morale in the NHS being low because of poor working conditions. Most organizations accept that low morale shows itself in higher rates of absenteeism and less job satisfaction. It is very important that those who look after your child are happy with their work. Childcarers who enjoy their work are much more likely to be warm and responsive to children's needs than those who don't really enjoy the work they do.

When you visit a nursery, apart from asking about staff turnover, check whether they are meeting basic staff needs – for example, nursery staff should have their own toilet or cloakroom, and a staff room where they can take a break from the children. As a parent, you will know how tiring it can be looking after one or two children for a few hours. Staff need some times during the day when they can spend time away from the children without fear of being interrupted. Taking a very short break, or no break at all, can mean that adults are less able to give children their best.

Regular staff meetings also help to create a friendly, supportive atmosphere among all nursery workers. It doesn't matter how big or small the nursery may be.

Providing continuity, and therefore good quality care, is often easier when one member of staff always works with the same small group of children. We often call this way of organizing nurseries the 'key worker system' – each member of staff has responsibility for several children whom they look after throughout their time in the nursery. The key worker system has several advantages for children, parents and staff. It gives children a chance to form a more stable relationship with an adult. We have already talked about the benefits of children feeling secure and safe with their adult carers. Feeling secure about a relationship with one adult in a nursery helps children feel happier and more confident about being away from their parents. A secure child is more likely to adapt to their nursery environment and get more out of it in terms of learning and development. Some children will have temporary problems with development. A key worker is more likely to notice possible difficulties than other staff, simply because they spend so much time with the individual children assigned to them.

Key workers are very useful sources of information for parents. Knowing your child's key worker means that you have someone you can talk to about your child's development. Having a special relationship with your child's professional carer is good for your child and good for you – you can be more confident that they are considering your wishes and concerns.

Staff are often much happier with key worker systems. It means they can develop rewarding relationships with the children in their care. Key workers can keep careful records of an individual child's development. These records help plan activities that fit closely with the needs of particular children at different stages.

Some nurseries argue that children get too attached to key workers, and that when their key worker is on holiday or falls ill, children can find it quite difficult. In these kinds of situations, it's helpful if the nursery can engage the same person or people to provide cover, so that the disruption to children caused by these absences is kept to a minimum.

There are several different ways of organizing key worker systems. In some nurseries, a key worker will spend most of their day with the same set of children. Organizing a system of care around this principle can be quite difficult. In other nurseries, the key worker will have responsibility for collecting information about a group of children, but will not necessarily spend all their time with them. It's worth asking how key worker systems operate in a nursery. Whatever the system, the thing to look for is consistency of care for children. On balance, it seems likely that the advantages of the key worker system firmly outweigh the disadvantages (see Box 6.3).

Information box 6.3: Advantages of 'key worker' systems

- More stable situation for children
- Progress of children carefully monitored
- Possible problems identified sooner
- Parents have one person they know they can talk to
- Parents more confident their wishes are being considered
- Staff find job more rewarding

Parents sometimes choose nursery care because, although staff may come and go, at least the nursery environment remains constant for the child, whereas changing childminders means both a change in carer and a change in the place where care is provided. However, this doesn't mean that nursery care is *always* better when it comes to continuity, but it does suggest that getting some idea about a childminder's future job plans is probably a good idea. For example, some mothers start childminding just to be at home until their own children start school. The childminder you choose could be someone who plans to stop minding before your child is ready to move on. It is certainly worth checking.

No matter how hard you try, a change of carer is sometimes unavoidable. Families move, childminders stop minding, nursery staff leave, and arrangements break down, or you may decide that your child is not receiving the quality of care you want. Although stability is extremely important, leaving a child in poor quality care is usually worse than the effect of a move. Where a change of carer is necessary, it will help if children are prepared for the changes that will take place.

Why is training for carers important for quality?

Usually, childcare workers who are well trained provide better quality care. That doesn't mean that all childcare workers without formal training provide poor quality care, it just means that you stand a better chance of getting good quality care for your child if the carer is properly trained. Well-trained carers respond more sensitively to young children's needs, are more aware of children's changing developmental needs, and encourage better peer interaction between children. Children generally do better in nurseries where staff have had more training. The Guidance to the Children Act recommends that at least half the care staff on duty at any one time should be professionally qualified.

Childcare workers can obtain several qualifications. Box 6.4 lists the more common ones. Courses vary in both length and intensity of training.

Childminders don't need to have formal childcare qualifications to be registered, but many local authorities now insist that childminders go on a short training course before they register them. The course is usually made up of several one- to two-hour sessions, covering topics such as health and safety, first aid, child protection, play/children's activities and equal opportunities.

Information box 6.4: Training for nursery workers

Qualification	Length of course	Age at entry
BTEC National Diploma in Caring Services (nursery nursing)	2 years full-time	16
National Nursery Examination Board certificate (NNEB)	2 yeas full-time	16
Certificate in Post-Qualifying Studies (CPQS)	Modular, part-time for those already professionally qualified	21
Pre-school Learning Alliance foundation course (PPA)	120 hours	Any
Initial teacher training (degree level)	4 years	18

Childminding today is becoming much more professional. Around half of all registered childminders belong to the National Childminding Association (NCMA). The NCMA does a great deal of work to help childminders offer a better service by providing support and training. The NCMA also recommends follow-on courses for newly-established childminders, and in-service training designed for experienced childminders.

Why is experience important for quality?

Experienced carers often provide better quality childcare. Some very good childcare workers have a great deal of experience of looking after children, but not so much in the way of formal qualifications. Bringing up a family, working in a playgroup or nursing are all examples of useful care experience. New ways for experienced people to get formal qualifications include work-based assessments, like National Vocational Qualifications (NVQs).

Although experience is important, it does very much depend on what kinds of experience carers have had. Bringing up a family is often not a sufficient qualification for a childcare worker. Having children doesn't make someone a good parent, just as buying a car doesn't make someone a good driver. Plenty of parents will admit that they don't have the skills, particularly the patience, to stay at home all day with young children. It's also worth remembering that looking after someone else's child is different from looking after your own.

Box 6.5 gives a checklist of questions to ask when assessing different care providers.

Information box 6.5: Continuity, training and experience – questions to ask

In the nursery:

- How many staff have left in the last year, and why?
- Is there a key worker system?
- What breaks do staff get during the day?
- Is there a staffroom away from the children?
- What arrangements are made to cover staff absences?
- Do at least half of your staff have childcare qualifications?

At the childminder's:

- How long do you intend to keep childminding?
- What training related to childcare do you have?
- Do you have a plan for alternative care if you are ill?

Equal opportunities policies in employment and service delivery

Why are equal opportunities important to quality?

A commitment to equal opportunities means being committed to the idea that a child or adult will not receive less favourable treatment on the grounds of their race, sex, colour, nationality, ethnic or national origins, sexual orientation, age, religion, marital status or disability. Having policies and practices that recognize issues of equal opportunities is an important aspect of good quality care. It's not just matters like numbers, colours and how to tie shoe laces that young children learn – children also learn about prejudice and stereotypes from adults. That's why it's important we give

children positive images of people whom we are often guilty of discriminating against. Equal opportunities policies should cover admissions and staff recruitment, as well as children's activities and the equipment provided for them.

Equal opportunities in admissions policies

All nurseries should have a written admissions policy based on equal opportunities criteria. This policy should set out how waiting lists are drawn up, and on what basis people are selected from them. Having selection priorities for different groups is very common, particularly in local authority and workplace nurseries. Nevertheless, for most nurseries, selecting children based on their race or gender is illegal.

The nursery should keep a record of admissions to make sure that they are following the principles of equal opportunities. The National Children's Bureau (NCB) suggests that records be kept on the sex and ethnic origin of all children applying to, offered places and attending the nursery. Nurseries should tell parents why they collect this kind of information – it is the only way they can check that their admissions practices are free from any racial or sex discrimination.

Equal opportunities in staff recruitment

The fact that most people working in nurseries are women can be a problem – it reinforces the idea that kind, caring behaviour is something that only women are good at, whereas many men are just as capable of providing good childcare. This kind of gender stereotyping can mean that working in nursery settings is not always easy for men. However, having a male member of staff has its advantages – for example, it can help encourage fathers to take a greater interest in the development of their child and the workings of the nursery.

Avoiding racial discrimination is just as important. Nurseries should think about how the mix of staff compares with the ethnic composition of the local community. In nurseries that have thought about equal opportunities, there should be few children attending the nursery who are from ethnic groups not represented on the staff. Having a multi-ethnic staff has other advantages. It always helps, for example, to have someone who can overcome language problems with members of the local community. Children learn best when we teach them in their first, or home, language, therefore recruiting care staff who can talk to children in their home language is important. A nursery employing staff from a variety of ethnic groups also provides children, parents and other staff with positive images of cultures other than their own.

Equal opportunities in children's activities and equipment

By the time children are 3, what they understand to be appropriate behaviour for boys and girls clearly influences their play. They reach this understanding from what they see or hear around them. That's why it's so important for professional childcarers to give children plenty of opportunities to see males and females in non-stereotypical roles. They need to be aware of the way they treat boys and girls.

Adults can give messages to children without realizing it. For example, girls often receive more cuddles than boys. In the same way, rough-and-tumble play is often more acceptable when boys are involved. Watch children in a childcare setting: are girls encouraged in construction or building activities, are boys encouraged to bathe and dress the doll? Think about what's being said to children. What message are children getting from comments like 'Annie, can you look after John?' or 'I need a strong boy to help me with this table,' or even 'Big boys don't cry'?

It is a fact that we live in a multicultural society. The importance of giving children positive images of people from cultures that are different to their own cannot be overemphasized. Nurseries and childminders are an invaluable resource when it comes to teaching children about different races and cultures. It doesn't matter whether you happen to live in a multicultural or largely white European community, the materials and equipment used by nurseries and childminders should reflect the diversity that is present in society. Very young children quickly pick up attitudes. The pictures children see in games, pictures, books and puzzles make a difference. Children need to see positive images of a variety of cultural groups. Racism affects children's development. Children need to feel good about people they can see are different from themselves. It helps them to feel good themselves.

Box 6.6 give a checklist of factors to consider in evaluating a care provider's equal opportunities policies.

Information box 6.6: Equal opportunities policies in employment and service delivery

Check that:

- there is a written admissions policy
- records are kept on admissions
- there is an equal opportunities policy
- the ethnic mix of staff reflects the local community
- adults give boys and girls similar opportunities
- posters and drawings show people from different races
- books, puzzles and games have pictures showing men and women in non-traditional roles
- festivals from other cultures are celebrated (for example, Chinese New Year, Diwali)

7
Activities in childcare settings

Ability to structure and support children's learning

Why is an ability to structure and support children's learning important to quality?

The move from childcare to school is a big step for both children and parents. Children starting school need a certain amount of self-confidence and independence. As a minimum, good quality childcare should provide a warm, safe and secure environment. On top of that, childcare can help to prepare children for the world of primary school. To do that, childcare providers need to take a systematic and structured approach to children's learning. This is particularly true for older children in childcare – the 3- and 4-year-olds. Providers should aim to teach certain basic skills to children about to start school.

Children may find starting school easier if they can do things like:

- dress and undress themselves
- take themselves to the toilet
- pay attention to stories or discussions
- name colours

Helping children to learn particular skills requires planning. Planning usually means having some sort of curriculum. To many people, a curriculum is appropriate to a school, not a nursery or childminder. Yet if children are going to get the most out of childcare, having a plan or a curriculum is important.

Having a curriculum does not mean organizing days into formal teaching sessions. Children under 5 are learning all the time. Counting while climbing stairs, naming colours of cars or playing with sand are all situations in which children are learning without adults doing any formal teaching. Children learn in informal ways. It often doesn't make sense to separate activities into either care or education. Consequently, some experts have come up with the word 'educare' to describe what goes on in childcare.

Play and other activities that are part of providing care can also be described as education. Having a curriculum helps nursery staff to plan activities. With a plan, staff can check that children of all ages have opportunities to develop the skills and abilities they need.

A report from the Department of Education and Science (DES, 1990) has pointed out that any curriculum for the under-fives should be based on the needs and characteristics of the children. Carers need to assess these needs and characteristics through a combination of observation, knowledge of child development and talking to parents.

Drawing up a curriculum can be done in many different ways. The report we mentioned suggests that a curriculum for young children should cover nine areas of experience and learning:

1 linguistic
2 aesthetic and creative
3 human and social
4 mathematical
5 moral
6 physical
7 scientific
8 technological
9 spiritual

So, for example, card and board games can help children learn about counting (mathematical), naming objects (linguistic) and taking turns (human/social). Playing outdoors with equipment like a see-saw could provide several learning experiences – for example, exercise (physical), helping children to learn about balancing (scientific) and reinforcing the idea that girls should be given the same opportunities for physical play as boys (moral).

As you can see from this short description, good curriculum planning takes time and requires quite a lot of thought – it's much more than just planning to get musical instruments out on Monday morning and paints out in the afternoon. Carers need to have a clear idea of which of the nine areas of experience and learning they want an activity to encourage. Next, they need to think how the chosen activity can achieve that. Just letting children play on a see-saw may not be enough to encourage learning about balancing. Adults will need to support the play by, for example, asking children to make guesses about which children would make the see-saw stay level or tip up.

An important part of using a curriculum successfully is keeping a check on progress. As staff put the plans into action, the reactions of children and staff need to be observed and recorded. Observations have to be brought back to the next planning meeting and used to change things in the light of everybody's

experiences. It is a continuous process of planning, doing, observ-
ing, assessing and then re-planning. This process should be part of
the day-to-day working of a nursery. In nurseries where they recognize curriculum planning as important, you will usually find
that they have planning sessions built into their weekly timetable.
It is definitely not good practice to expect staff to plan and prepare
activities at the end of a hard day working with children.

A weekly timetable describing activities
for each group of children should be on
display for everyone to see. That way care
staff and parents can see that children
are experiencing a good range of activities designed to help them learn the skills
they need.

In most nurseries offering full-time care, the day is made up of
periods of play divided by times for regular routine activities, such
as hand washing, snacks, lunch and rest. Daily routines are important – they provide children (and adults too) with a sense of
security and familiarity. However, adults need to be flexible when
the situation calls for it – for example, they might allow children
to continue making models after lunch, even if they have planned
another activity. Changing a planned activity at the beginning
of the day to take account of children's moods or interests is
obviously a good idea. This kind of flexibility means that adults
can respond to new opportunities for learning as and when they
crop up.

It's often beneficial for nurseries to have good contacts with
local schools. Talking to teachers at the new school should be part
of any planning exercise aimed at helping children who are about
to leave the nursery. Workplace nurseries, because they often look
after children who do not live locally, may not always be well
placed to make links with schools.

Childminders often need to plan activities in a similar way to nurseries. Of course, they don't have the same facilities at home as nurseries do, but they can offer children just as wide a range of activities by using playgroups, drop-in centres and the like to support their learning. As we noted earlier, with good planning, every-day activities in the home can be turned into exciting and interesting learning opportunities for children. Just think how many different skills can be built into an activity like baking a few buns.

Many childminders also have good contacts with local schools. Because they are dropping off and collecting older children, they have an opportunity to talk to teachers and to introduce children in their care to the new environment.

Box 7.1 gives a checklist you can use to gauge how well the care provider structures and supports children's learning.

Information box 7.1: Structuring and supporting children's learning

Check that:

- there is a planned curriculum
- activities are organized with learning objectives in mind
- there is a good range of activities on offer
- time for staff to plan is built into the working day
- the curriculum is on display for all to see
- there is a clear idea of the skills children need when starting school
- there are good contacts with local schools

Elements in programme of activities

What elements in a programme of activities are important to quality?

A good quality childcare setting will offer children a variety of activities. Variety is important in keeping children interested, but it is also essential because children need to learn such a wide range of skills in their early years.

Parents often think children in childcare spend too much time playing and not enough time being taught. Professional care workers certainly think that parents want to see their children involved in more educational activities which prepare them for school. Of course, parents want their children to do well, but when it comes to children's activities, we need to understand the importance of play.

There are two important things to remember about play. First, it's fun! All children, no matter what their age, enjoy playing. Second, children learn an awful lot through play – for example, playing with a puzzle can teach a child about colour and shape. Playing in the sand can teach children about weight, about touch, even about maths. Children playing with a ball are learning about  balance, eye-to-hand co-ordination and the pleasures of sharing activities. Play gives children a chance to use their imagination and to be creative.

Dividing children's activities into either play or education just doesn't make sense. Decades of research in many different countries have shown how children learn through play. Because play is fun, children get used to the idea that learning is fun. What better start could we give children? Starting school with the idea that learning is fun gives children a positive attitude to education. Children are more likely to get the most out of school when they enjoy it.

Box 7.2 sets out some of the elements in a well-thought out programme of activities.

Children's involvement in planning and choosing activities and projects

Why is children's involvement in planning important to quality?

Involving children in the planning of an activity provides opportunities for the development of language and reasoning skills – for example, a group of children may discuss what they will need for a cooking activity later in the day, or make plans for an outing. This gives children a sense of having some control in their daily activities, and it helps them to learn about making decisions. It's difficult to say at what age children should be involved in planning activities – it depends on the individual child – but certainly the 3- and 4-year-olds need to be encouraged to plan activities.

Giving children the chance to choose an activity for themselves helps to promote independence. It gives children responsibility for deciding how they will spend their time. Choice helps children to learn about the consequences of their actions. Carers can give children choices by getting out more than one

Information box 7.2: What children learn from a good programme of activities

Activity	Necessary equipment	Children can learn about
Physical play	Bats, balls, bean bags, wheeled toys slides, swings, climbing frames	Throwing, catching, balancing, kicking, sharing, co-ordination, etc.
Imaginative play	Dressing-up clothes, dolls, kitchen toys, boxes, sheets, other household oddments	Language, co-operation, numbers, roles (police officer, firefighter), etc.
Toys and games	Books, puzzles, bricks, cards	Colour, shape, manipulating small objects, language, numbers, turn-taking, sharing, etc.
Creative play	Paints, crayons, glue, playdough, cardboard, scissors, small bits of junk	Shape, size, textures, colour, eye-to-hand co-ordination, construction, etc.
Sand and water play	Sand tray or sand pit, water tray, cups, buckets, spades, jugs	Size, shape, number, textures, co-operation, wet/dry, etc.
Music and movement	Rattles, drums, tambourines, shakers, tapes, records, toy instruments	Sound, rhythm, co-operation, singing, language

toy, game or other activity at a time. Allowing children to choose from a range of alternatives – like art, books, puzzles and imaginative play – provides choice. For infants and younger children, offering a range of playthings such as rattles, posting boxes, mirrors and soft toys gives them a choice about what to play with.

It's often easier for adults if they tell children what they can do and which materials they can use. The problem with this approach is that it doesn't help children to learn about making decisions for themselves. We sometimes call the kinds of adult-directed activities you will see in a nursery 'group time'. What to look for is a mix of group time and periods during which children have a choice of activities. It may not make life easy for adults if one child wants to paint while another wants to read, but again, good quality childcare is not just about what is easy for adults.

Elements of imagination, challenge and adventure in activities

Why are elements of imagination, challenge and adventure in activities important to quality?

Good quality childcare helps children to develop. Children learn most when they are interested and excited by what they are doing. Falling into stale routines can be very easy for professional carers. We all do it. Once you've found some activity children enjoy, the temptation is to repeat it again and again, without ever changing it. The use of television is probably the most common example. Children enjoy watching videos and television programmes. Some can be quite educational if adults use them as part of planned learning activities – for example, they could link a programme about animals to art, pretend and creative play later in the day. But a group of children sat in front of a TV supervised by a single, silent adult is not a good example of an imaginative or exciting activity.

Making sure that children's activities are imaginative, challenging and adventurous requires planning. Unless professional carers spend time planning what they are going to do with children, it's less likely they can maintain their interest. Have a look for a timetable posted up somewhere in a nursery. Good planning will usually mean that the timetable is different each week. You don't want to see a timetable that's been up for weeks without being changed. Another good sign is a timetable that says a bit more than 'outside play' or 'art' or some other general activity. The more specific the timetable is, the more likely some thoughtful planning has gone into it. Although childminders may not display timetables in their homes, they should be able to tell you about the range of activities they have provided over the last week or two.

You can usually tell something about the quality of planned activities by looking at nursery displays – too many commercially-made posters is a bad sign. Children's drawings, models or other work should make up most of what's on display. Look for themes running through work – such as 'autumn' or 'animals' or any simple idea that children can understand. Pictures on display don't all have to look the same. Children get more out of doing their own thing, rather than making simple copies of something an adult has done. Twenty versions of a paper plate with bits of pasta stuck on to make a face is often a sign that not much imagination has gone into the activity. The same goes for a childminder's home. Although you wouldn't expect works of art displayed on every wall, you should be able to see some examples of children's work. Children's own imagination should not be restricted just because adults may lack inspiration.

Have a look for some evidence that the provider takes children on trips or outings. Photographs of 'our day at the park' or 'our trip to the seaside' are something else to look for.

8
The physical environment

Organization, display and accessibility of equipment, toys and materials

Why is organization of materials important to quality?

We often overlook the importance of storage when considering the features of good childcare. There should be sufficient storage space to allow equipment, toys and materials to be easily accessible to children, not kept on high shelves or in drawers that can't be opened easily. Organizing materials in this way may not be as easy for childminders working in their own homes. Some childminders get around this problem by having a special children's area or room. Others simply accept that, during the day at least, their homes are child-centred environments first, and 'ideal homes' second.

Usually, the more storage space there is, the more activities children have to choose from. It's also easier for staff to check that they have enough of everything when they can see easily what the nursery does and doesn't have.

Imposing some order on how equipment is stored will help children learn where it belongs – it gives a sense of permanence and helps children learn skills such as classifying, sorting, assigning a place to things and memory of the place. These are all important skills for the development of children's reasoning and later learning. Labelling the container or shelf with both a word and a picture of the contents serves two purposes – it helps younger children find where equipment belongs, and it helps older children with word recognition.

Research has shown that organized storage seems to produce more complex and longer-lasting play. From the adult's point of view, organization may encourage the use of a wide range of different materials, rather than a limited range which is close to hand. Box 8.1 gives a checklist of factors to look out for.

Information box 8.1: Organization of materials

Check that:

- there is enough storage space for all toys and equipment
- drawers, shelves, etc. are labelled with a word and a picture
- children can help themselves to toys, books, puzzles, etc.
- there is enough of everything, so children don't have to wait too long for their turn
- adults ensure children have a variety of things to play with
- older children are encouraged to put things away

In their first five years, children's developmental needs change rapidly. They need a variety of equipment and materials appropriate for their age and ability, so variety is important. Providing only a limited range of materials means less challenge and less interest for children. Some carers will say that giving children a choice simply confuses them. That's not true. Often it's just an excuse so that adults can avoid the bother of getting out a full range of equipment.

Having too little play equipment can often lead to more aggressive behaviour in children, mainly as a result of children fighting over toys or games. Having a good supply of equipment benefits both adults and children – adults spend less time sorting out fights, and children spend more time actively engaged and less time waiting for their turn. Older children should be encouraged to share or take their turn on a particular piece of equipment. Younger children (6 months to 2 years) simply don't have the intellectual and emotional skills needed to understand the idea of sharing. Providing lots of similar toys and games definitely helps.

Attention to health, safety and type of physical environment

Why is attention to health, safety and type of physical environment important to quality?

Children need a safe and healthy environment. It is an essential component of good quality care. Unsafe or unhealthy environments put children at risk. Accidents are the most common cause of death among toddlers and older children. Every day, four children in the UK die as the result of accidents. Nobody wants to see children hurt, but minor accidents are part of growing up. Most cannot be avoided. However, paying attention to simple rules of health and safety can avoid serious accidental injuries.

Young children often have accidents simply because they don't know what is or isn't dangerous – a 2-year-old would not understand the dangers of poking a pencil into an electric socket, for example. Children don't always understand when adults tell them about dangers. Their natural curiosity and desire to explore can lead them into dangerous situations. Adults often underestimate a child's abilities – dangerous items and equipment that we think are out of reach are often not. The simple rule is that if they can't find an interesting, safe place to play, children will play in places that are dangerous.

Because childminders work in their own homes, safety is particularly important. That's not to say that parents shouldn't make similar checks in nurseries. Even something simple like placing covers over unused electric sockets can sometimes be forgotten. We could probably fill a whole book with health and safety information. The best we can do here is to go over some more common problems for you.

Indoors

To prevent accidents and the risk of fire, electrical equipment must be safe. There should only be one plug per socket. Electrical flexes must not be frayed or bare. Cables should be fixed to the wall or secured so that children cannot reach them or trip over them. Safety (shutter-type) sockets should be fitted in areas accessible to children, and covers should be fitted to sockets not in use.

Glass doors, windows or tables can be sources of danger. When ordinary glass smashes, it breaks into lots of long, sharp pieces. Safety glass is not just stronger, it is less dangerous when it breaks. Safety film is clear plastic film which can be stuck to one side of the glass. If the glass breaks, the film stops broken pieces going everywhere.

Children shouldn't be able to get onto balconies. Remember

other areas too, like cellars, attics, garages, roofs and sheds – they should all be impossible for children to gain access to unless supervised.

Most local authorities will insist that childminders have smoke alarms fitted in their homes. Alarms and firefighting equipment are very important in nurseries. Regular fire drills are essential to make sure that staff know how and when this equipment should be used.

One of the quickest ways of spreading infection or contagious diseases is to share personal items like towels. Nurseries and childminders should either provide disposable towels or give each child their own towel. The same applies to adults. They should not share towels with the children.

The area where children sleep or rest should be peaceful, dimly-lit and kept at a comfortable temperature. Quiet and softness are the key considerations for good quality nap time. Each child should have a cot, mattress or large cushion to lie on. The amount of time children need to sleep or rest varies according to their age and their individual needs, as does the time of day. Most toddlers and preschoolers may be ready to nap after lunch, some children may want to sleep or rest during the morning or afternoon, while others may not wish to or need to sleep. Providers should respect their choice. Children often find it difficult to lie quietly or sleep when they do not feel tired. Some nurseries offer children alternatives – those who do not want a nap can sit or lie quietly and look at books. Meeting the needs of individual children is an important aspect of good quality care.

Outdoors

Outdoor play areas can be a particular source of danger. Children need space to run around, play ball games and pedal bikes without getting in each others' way. A playground that's too small puts children at greater risk of having accidents. Nurseries without a large play area need to organize time outdoors for small groups.

It's an asset if childminders have their own garden for children to play in, but not essential – children can be taken to the local park. They should not be able to get out of a garden unsupervised. A fence at least 1.2 metres (about 4 feet) high is usually enough, but it should not provide footholds that children could use to climb over it. The garden gate should be self-closing and fitted with either a childproof lock or a lock that is out of reach.

Physical layout

The organization of space affects the behaviour of both adults and children. The same is true for both nurseries and childminders' homes.

Having activity areas clearly marked helps children to keep materials in the same place. Children are less likely to get distracted, and so find it easier to concentrate on what they are doing. Corners set aside for different play materials help children carry out simple instructions like 'Put the book back in the book corner'. This encourages independence. Setting up activity areas, either permanently or temporarily, in the same place in the room gives children a sense of security and competence. Creating designated areas is possible, though there may not be enough space for them to be permanent.

Spending all day in a group setting can be very demanding for children, so they also need a place where they can get a bit of peace and quiet, and where they do not have to talk to people unless they want to – for example, reading or looking at books should be possible without distractions. Care providers can arrange furniture so that it effectively screens part of the room off to create a corner away from the general traffic flow and group activities. A quiet corner needs to feel restful, and should have comfortable seating, such as cushions, bean bags, a mattress or, if there is room, a sofa or armchair. A rug or carpet adds to the feeling of cosiness and helps to reduce noise. The space should create a feeling of warmth and safety.

Having ample space for children to play freely is important. Too little space will result in children getting in each other's way, and this affects their play. If children disturb each other's play, it's more likely that trouble will start between them. Accidents are also more likely, particularly if there is a wide age range in the group. Restricted space also limits the choice of activities available to children, which in turn may lead to boredom and frustration. It is no surprise that having insufficient space, either in the nursery or in the home, leads to less adult–child interaction and more adult control and restriction. Children become aimless and bored, less co-operative with other children, more aggressive, and less involved in games requiring concentration

Infants

Weather permitting, infants gain a lot from being outside – it's a chance for them to watch and explore the surroundings outside their nursery room. A clean, soft surface, like a rug or blanket, can provide a safe, healthy and comfortable area for infants. It allows some freedom of movement, which is important for infants who are learning about different parts of their bodies and how they work.

Equipment like pushchairs or baby walkers can be useful in caring for infants and toddlers. Nevertheless, they are sometimes used more for the benefit of adults than children. In fact, some organizations do not recommend baby walkers (for example, the Child Accident Prevention Trust) – babies can move very fast in a walker, which makes them difficult to supervise, they can cause accidents, and they don't help children learn to walk. Cots, playpens, highchairs, etc., can become a prison from the child's point of view. They should only be used for very short periods, because they restrict movement and the opportunity to explore. Young children in this situation quickly become bored, and may fall asleep or become irritable. Of course, an active infant or toddler is usually free from danger if confined, which allows adults to get on with other things. However, leaving infants or toddlers restricted in this way for lengthy periods is a misuse of the equipment.

Box 8.2 provides a checklist of examples of health and safety considerations.

Information box 8.2: Health, safety and the physical environment

Check that:

- all electric sockets are covered or out of reach
- children can't get into dangerous areas (for example, the kitchen)
- individual or disposable towels are supplied for children and adults
- there is a fully-stocked first aid box
- one member of staff is fully trained in first aid
- children can't get out of an outdoor play area
- activity areas are well marked
- there is a quiet corner for children to sit in
- there is enough space for children to play freely

Part three

Part three of *Choosing Childcare* looks at the practical problems of finding childcare. It tells you how to find childminders and nurseries, how to choose a place that suits you and your child, and how to make the arrangement work.

Before you begin your search, it helps to list the things to ask and look for – in this way, you won't forget something important. You are also less likely to discover later something which is unacceptable to you. Part two described the 13 areas to look for in good quality care. In part three, we provide a set of guiding questions to help you decide whether the childcare provider offers care of a high standard. Although we have focused on childminders and day nurseries, you can use some of this information when looking for other forms of preschool provision, such as playgroups.

This part of the book has three chapters:

- Chapter 9 – How to find a good childminder
- Chapter 10 – How to find a good nursery
- Chapter 11 – Making childcare work

9
How to find a good childminder

This chapter tells you when and where you can look for a childminder. It includes a list of questions you will need to ask. You will also find a list of things to look for in a childminder's home that can give you clues about the quality of care she is providing.

When to begin

Start looking as soon as you can. Some parents begin to search even before their baby is born. This may seem a bit early, but do give yourself plenty of time to choose a childminder. An early start is especially important if the mother plans to go back to work within a few months after the birth. A new baby will take up most of your time and energy. You can avoid having to look for a childminder in these first weeks by simply thinking ahead.

Making an early start can give you more choice. You won't have to settle for second best just because you've run out of time. If you do find a good childminder ahead of time, you may have to pay a retainer. A retainer is just like a deposit – the childminder will keep a place open until your child is ready to start. Paying a retainer or deposit is a way of letting the childminder know that you are serious about taking up the place. If you change your mind, the childminder usually keeps the retainer. The money goes some way towards making up for any inconvenience and loss of income.

Where to begin

Start with your local authority. The Children Act says that local authorities must keep a list of all registered childminders in their area. Contact the person responsible for childminders – their job title may vary in different authorities, but usually they are called the 'under-eights adviser/officer', or 'childcare co-ordinator'. They usually work in a Social Services department, which will be in the town hall or an area office. Don't be surprised if you have to speak to more than one person before contacting the one you want!

The under-eights adviser can probably give you the names, addresses and telephone numbers of childminders with vacancies living in your area. Remember what we said in part two of the book: these are not lists of *recommended* childminders. The law says that local authorities must register *all* childminders. The list simply gives details of all registered childminders in your area.

Social Services departments vary in the way they compile their childminder lists. For instance, some lists will tell you about the number and ages of children a registered childminder can care for, whether she smokes, and if she has any pets. However, this sort of information – particularly information about vacancies – can change quite quickly, and childminders who stop or take a break from working don't always let Social Services departments know about these changes, so keeping a completely up-to-date list can be difficult. Some departments will only give you the names of three or four child-minders at a time – if none are available or suitable, you have to ask for another batch of names. If you can't find a childminder living near you, think about other conve-nient areas – for example, you might find someone who lives on your route to work, or close to your office. This may mean having to get in touch with another Social Services department in a different authority. Ask the adviser to give you as many names in as many places as possible. Some local authorities run childminding vacancy schemes. They divide the authority into small areas. In each area, one childminder acts as a co-ordinator, who keeps an up-to-date list of the childminders living in their area. Childminders notify them when they have a vacancy or when a vacancy has been filled. Parents can often obtain more up-to-date lists from local co-ordinators, which makes this service extremely helpful. If nothing else, it cuts down on time making phone calls. Social Services departments may give you the names and tele-phone numbers of area co-ordinators.

Childminders often get together in support groups and net-works. These groups usually have information about vacancies. Your Social Services department or the National Childminding Association will give you details of any groups in your area.

Finally, don't forget that word-of-mouth or recommendation is often a good way of finding a childminder. Ask your friends, rela-tives, health visitor or GP: they can probably recommend some-one. The more people who know you are looking for a childminder the better.

Visiting a prospective childminder

Once you have a list of the names, you will need to telephone them. Make sure each childminder you talk to is still registered and still minding. When you contact a childminder for the first time, most will want to know:

- your child's age
- the hours and days when you require care (for example, 8.30 a.m. to 5.45 p.m., Monday to Thursday)
- when you want the arrangement to start

Find out about a few more details before deciding whether you want to visit the childminder at home – seeking basic information during a phone call can save you time. You probably don't want to visit a childminder who doesn't fulfil your list of essential requirements (see Chapter 3). For example, you could ask about the number of children she currently minds, their ages, whether she smokes, and what (if any) training she has had. Obviously, if you are telephoning during the day, the childminder is likely to have children around, so keeping her talking on the phone is probably not a good idea – you can always arrange to call back at a more convenient time.

You won't be able to tell whether a childminder is suitable without visiting her at home. It is vital to visit at least once before making a final decision, and if possible, try to make several visits before you do so. Good childminders will want you to visit them, and most would not agree to take your child without meeting you both. Make a visit even if friends have recommended the childminder to you – what suits one parent doesn't always suit another.

You should try to make one visit when the children being cared for are around. If you make more than one visit, try to arrange them for different times of the day. For example, visiting at lunchtime or during a play session can tell you different things about how the childminder works with children.

Most parents admit feeling a little anxious on a first visit, which is quite understandable. Parents often have anxieties about sharing the care of their child with someone else. Childminders generally understand these anxieties. Some will even encourage you to talk a little about how you feel.

Use the initial meeting to form a few first impressions. Box 9.1 tells you about the kind of important information you can find out quickly and easily. If first impressions are good, you can find out more, possibly during another visit. This is a time for talking – for asking and answering questions about your childcare needs. Take along your list of questions and things to look for, and don't be afraid to use it. An experienced childminder will expect and even encourage you to ask questions. All the same, try not to turn it into an interrogation – you can obtain a lot of this information in the course of a friendly chat. Although the childminder may have more experience of first-time meetings with parents, it's quite natural for her to feel a little anxious too.

Information box 9.1: Areas to explore on a first visit to a childminder

On a first visit, you can often find out:

- if there is enough space for children to play
- where children sleep or rest
- if children are happy there
- how the childminder responds to children
- what security arrangements have been made
- if the childminder smokes
- what pets they have

The childminder will need to know a little about your child and family – for example, your child's health, behaviour, what they like and dislike, and their sleeping routines. This kind of information can help a childminder provide the best possible care for your child. The childminder will also want to know your views on childcare, and how you see the childminding arrangement working. Just as you have to decide whether you can get along with them, the childminder has to decide whether she thinks she can work with you and your child. She also needs to be confident that you and your child will fit in with the service she provides for other parents and children. Childminding is about working with parents and with children. The relationship between childminder and parent can be as important as the relationship between childminder and child.

You may be very lucky and decide that the first childminder you visit is the right one for you. Even so, it's probably a good idea to visit another – you can only make comparisons if you have visited several childminders, and making notes during your visits will help you decide which is best for you.

There's no need to hide the fact that you're planning to visit other childminders. In a small area, word will soon get out that you are doing the rounds. Nevertheless, if you've visited a childminder and said you would get back to them, it is only polite to do so, even if it's only to tell them that you have made other arrangements.

It's often difficult for parents to know what questions they should ask a childminder, so we've drawn up a list of 20 questions. Have a look at the list below and decide which ones you think are most important for you. You will probably find that you don't really need to ask all 20. If you ask each childminder you visit the same questions, you will find it easier to decide which childminder to choose. We've also set out these questions in Box 9.2 in the form of a checklist which you could take along on your visit.

Information box 9.2: Checklist for assessing a childminder

Twenty questions to ask a childminder

1	How long do you intend to continue minding?	OK	Not sure
2	Will other adults be around when my child is here?	OK	Not sure
3	How many children do you look after?	OK	Not sure
4	How long have you been looking after the children you mind now?	OK	Not sure
5	Have you been able to go on any training courses?	OK	Not sure
6	Are you a member of the NCMA?	OK	Not sure
7	Do you have links with other childminders in the area?	OK	Not sure
8	What is your daily routine?	OK	Not sure
9	What do you enjoy doing most with the children?	OK	Not sure
10	How often do you go out with the children?	OK	Not sure
11	Do you take the children out in your car?	OK	Not sure
12	What are the most important things you provide for children?	OK	Not sure
13	What are your views on toilet training?	OK	Not sure

14	How do you handle discipline?	OK	Not sure
15	How do you fit in chores and your family with your childminding?	OK	Not sure
16	What kind of food do you provide for the children?	OK	Not sure
17	Do you have insurance cover?	OK	Not sure
18	Do you have a settling-in policy?	OK	Not sure
19	What arrangements have you made for emergencies?	OK	Not sure
20	Are you prepared to look after children with special needs?	OK	Not sure

Ten things to look for

1	Is the house clean?	OK	Not sure
2	Is the house safe?	OK	Not sure
3	Is there an outside play space?	OK	Not sure
4	Is the outside area safe?	OK	Not sure
5	Are there plenty of toys for children to play with?	OK	Not sure
6	Are the toys appropriate for ages of children?	OK	Not sure
7	Can you see evidence that she values cultural differences?	OK	Not sure
8	Does she seem to have a warm, caring relationship with the children?	OK	Not sure

9	Do children seem happy, content and involved in what they are doing?	OK	Not sure
10	How does she talk about other parents and children?	OK	Not sure

Before you start, just remember that you are talking to a child-minder, not interviewing a murder suspect! Ask your questions in a friendly way. Both you and the childminder should feel relaxed with each other – that way, you are more likely to get the information you are looking for.

Twenty questions to ask a childminder

1   *How long do you intend to continue minding?* If you are looking for a place until your child goes to school, you don't want a childminder who plans to stop within a year or so.

2   *Will other adults be around (the childminder's husband, own children, friends) when my child is here?* If so, it is important to find out who they are and how they feel about the child-minding. If they will be involved in the care of children, meeting and talking to them is vital.

3   *How many children do you look after?* A childminder may look after lots of children on a part-time basis. That can mean a great deal of coming and going, with different children being around on different days. You may want to think about how that might affect your child if you are considering a full-time place.

4   *How long have you been looking after the children you mind now?*
Having some idea about the turnover of children can tell
you something about the childminder. If children do not stay
very long, there may be a problem. Find out where children
have moved to. Some parents use a childminder for a short
time while they wait for a nursery place, in which case, high
turnover of children is no cause for worry. Nevertheless,
parents don't usually move their children from one childminder to another unless problems have arisen.

5   *Have you been able to go on any training courses to do with childcare?* Experience as a parent doesn't always guarantee good
quality childminding. Looking after other people's children
is different from looking after your own. Training provides
practical information and advice to help childminders offer
a high standard of care.

6   *Are you a member of the NCMA?* The NCMA (National
Childminding Association) is a valuable resource for childminders. They provide good quality information, support
and advice. The NCMA also offers its members special
insurance rates. Membership of the NCMA suggests that the
childminder takes their work seriously.

7   *Do you have links with other childminders in the area?*
Childminding can be a lonely job. Although working with
children can be very pleasant, a complete lack of adult conversation, day in day out, would drive many of us round the
bend. Contact with other childminders offers a chance to
swap ideas and share problems. Support groups can be particularly useful if emergencies crop up.

8   *What is your daily routine?* Try to gain some idea of what the

childminder does with the children during the day. Does she find time to read, play with and talk to all the children? How long are children left in play pens, high chairs or baby walkers? How often do children watch TV? What do they watch?

9   *What do you enjoy doing most with the children?* There are no right or wrong answers to this question. Nevertheless, a childminder who finds this hard to answer may not do very much with the children.

10   *How often do you go out with the children?* Some childminders have to make as many as four trips to the local school each day. For a toddler, that can mean a lot of time spent in a pushchair. Other childminders rarely take children out. Does she use toddler groups, playgroups, etc., that may be in the area?

11   *Do you take the children out in your car?* If the childminder takes the children on special outings, where do they go, and how do they get there? Does she use her car and, if so, are car seats/seat belts used? Does she have insurance cover to use her car for this purpose?

12   *What are the most important things you hope to provide for the children you look after?* The answer to this question will give you some idea of the childminder's aims and ideas about childminding. Think about how her ideas fit in with your own.

13   *What are your views on toilet training?* However much you want a childminder to be just like you, it is very unlikely that you will find such a person. Finding a childminder who has views about child rearing that are similar to yours will help.

The chances are the arrangement will be less of a problem if the childminder holds views that aren't very different from your own.

14 *How do you handle discipline?* Ask how she handles temper tantrums, fighting over toys and games, or a child who refuses to co-operate.

15 *How do you fit household chores and the demands of a family in with your childminding work?* A childminder's priority should be the children in her care. Some childminders do housework before the children arrive or at the weekend. Others do it during the day, but involve the children in the activity. Household chores can be good opportunities for learning, especially if the childminder chats to the children about what they are doing – for example, helping to put shopping away can teach children about shape (square boxes, round tins), counting, colour and naming (vegetables, fruit or other foods).

16 *What kind of food do you provide for the children?* Does the childminder give children a varied and well-balanced diet? How does she react if children don't want to eat what she has served up? Are mealtimes at a regular time? Does she hold infants when feeding them? Does she mind babies getting in a mess when learning to feed themselves?

17 *Do you have insurance that covers you if children have an accident or cause damage to property while in your care?* Placing a child with a childminder who was not insured would be very unwise. Ask to see an insurance certificate.

18 *Do you have a settling-in policy?* Can parents introduce chil-

dren gradually into the new arrangement? For example, can you spend a few hours with your child before leaving them on their own for short periods. If a childminder isn't keen on the idea, it may mean that she will not always be sensitive to the needs of either you or your child. How would she handle a child who cries for their parents?

19 *What arrangements have you made in case of an emergency?* Does the childminder have any back-up plans? For example, if there was an emergency involving her own children, and she had to rush out to the hospital, what would she do with the children she minds?

20 *Are you prepared to look after children with special needs?* If your child has special needs, you will want some idea of the skills and understanding she has when it comes to looking after your child.

What do I need to look for?

As well as the information you can obtain by talking to a child-minder, you can learn a lot by watching, looking and listening. Below is a list of ten things you may want to look out for. They are also set out in the checklist in Box 9.2.

1 *Is the house clean?* Ask to see all the rooms that children use, including the bathroom. Does the house seem organized or chaotic? Is it too tidy or too dirty? Neither of these is acceptable for young children.

2 *Is the house safe?* Are there any safety hazards? For example, check fires, stairs, electrical appliances and sockets, all of

which can be dangerous. Are there covers on electric sockets not in use?

3   *Is there an outside play space?* Check for yourself.

4   *Is the outside area safe?* Could children get out if they were left alone for a few minutes? Are there any dangerous plants or features (like a pond) that could be a danger? How does the childminder supervise outdoor play?

5   *Are there plenty of different toys and activities for children to play with?* Toys should be in good repair – not broken or with pieces missing. If you see a box of toys, ask if there are other toys for children to play with. Some childminders bring out different toys at different times. On the other hand, the same box of toys may not change from one year to the next. If the childminder shows you a room full of toys belonging to her children, be sure to check that minded children can also play with them.

6   *Are the toys provided appropriate for the ages of children being looked after?* As well as looking for variety and amount, check that play materials are suitable for the ages of the minded children. For example, toddlers will want more than infant toys to play with.

7   *Can you see any evidence that she values cultural differences?* Look at picture books, picture puzzles, card or board games. Do they include pictures of people from different cultures? The same applies to pretend play props (clothes, dolls, puppets, Lego people, home corner items).

8   *Does she seem to have a warm and caring relationship with the*

children she cares for? Do children seem comfortable around the childminder? Do they come to her for help, comfort or reassurance? How does she talk to children?

9   *Do children seem happy, content and involved in what they are doing?* Children shouldn't be bored, be staring vacantly into space, be wandering around with nothing to do, or unnaturally quiet. Nor should they look miserable or afraid. Watch to see if children are hesitant or look nervously at the childminder when they are playing – this behaviour might suggest that the childminder is too strict.

10 *How does she talk about other parents and children?* Is she mainly positive in the way she speaks about parents and children? Does she seem supportive and understanding?

Should I take my child along on the first visit to a childminder?

Some parents like to make the first visit on their own. Having the distraction of a child can make it more difficult to concentrate on asking the right questions. Deciding whether you are likely to get on with someone who will be looking after your child is very important. Of course, you also need to be sure that your child is going to get along with the childminder, and you can only do that by watching the two of them together. Look for how the childminder takes an interest in your child. No matter what their age, does she talk to them, smile, encourage them to play and ask what they like to do? At some point before you decide, you will need to visit the childminder's home with your child.

Finalizing the arrangement – signing a contract

Once you've found a childminder you are happy with, finalize the arrangement as soon as possible – the vacancy may be filled if you wait. You will need to agree on a fee, including over-time, holidays, sickness and hours as well as the items listed in Box 9.3. When it comes to hours, be honest – don't agree to drop-off and pick-up times that you know you probably cannot keep. Arriving early or late on a regular basis is almost guaranteed to annoy the most patient of childminders.

No matter how good a relationship you think you have with your childminder, make sure you both sign a written contract. Goodwill is not enough to sort out problems should they arise. Most childminders and professional organizations involved with childminding agree that written contracts are a good idea. Why? Because you can forget details of an agreement, because a written document makes it easier to sort out problems, and because written contracts put childminding on a more professional footing.

You should agree on written contracts even if you have known the childminder as a friend, or someone you trust has recommended them. Having a formal written contract doesn't mean you don't really trust this person – it shows that you recognize the importance of the job a childminder does and respect their status as a professional childcarer. Both the National Childminding Association and many local authorities provide standard contract forms for childminders to use. If you choose to draw up your own contract, Box 9.3 tells you what you need to include.

Information box 9.3: A childminding contract

A contract with a childminder should include:

- starting date
- agreed drop-off and pick-up times
- days the child will be minded
- fees, including rates for overtime
- charges for

  - sickness
  - occasional days off
  - child's holidays
  - childminder's holidays
  - bank holidays

- when payment is due
- who pays for extras such as playgroup fees
- the names of people who may collect your child
- period of notice
- what parents agree to supply
- other special arrangements
- date for review

Both you and the childminder should sign and date the contract and each of you should keep a copy. Any changes to the agreement – for example, the days when your child attends – should be changed on the contract. It's helpful to review the contract regularly, say every six months or every year, to check that everyone is happy with the agreement and to discuss changes that you may need to make. It also helps to know at the beginning of the agreement when and how frequently the childminder reviews her fees.

If a childminder is reluctant to sign a contract, you should think very carefully before entering into the arrangement. A contract is no guarantee that you will easily resolve problems, but it does establish the ground rules.

10
How to find a good nursery

This chapter tells you when and where to look for a nursery place. It includes a list of questions you will need to ask. You will also find a list of things to look for in a nursery that can give you clues about the quality of care being provided.

When to begin

In most areas, the demand for nursery places far outweighs the supply, so you cannot start your search too soon. Most nurseries that offer childcare for working parents have long waiting lists. If you have more than one nursery to choose from, it might be a good idea to put your name on more than one list, but this won't guarantee a place will be available just when you need it. This is particularly true if you are seeking a baby place. Have an alternative plan – for example, you may have to use a relative or childminder while you wait for a nursery place to become available. If you've organized an alternative, you're less likely to be caught out if your chosen nursery closes or changes in character before you need a place.

Where to begin

Each local authority keeps a register of nurseries in their area. The Social Services department will usually send you a list. You need to speak to the person responsible for registering day nurseries – usually the childcare co-ordinator or under-eights adviser. Alternatively, your local library keeps a list too. Some authorities will provide additional information, such as opening hours and the age range catered for. Remember, this is only a list of registered nurseries. It is *not* a list of approved or recommended nurseries.

Once you've chosen possible nurseries, call and ask them to send you information about the place. This may range from a glossy brochure to a photocopied sheet. Try not to be influenced by the quality of the brochure you receive – it's the information in the brochure that's most important. Start by looking at matters like opening hours and whether the nursery operates throughout the year or only during school term times, whether they offer full-time and/or part-time places, the age range of children they cater for, whether children must be toilet trained before starting, and of course, fees. If the nursery doesn't have any paperwork to send out, you'll have to obtain this information during a phone call or brief visit.

Visiting a prospective nursery

Never select a nursery without visiting the premises. You must go and see for yourself. Recommendations are useful, but they are no substitute for a visit. Visit more than one nursery – you may be very pleased with the look of the first one you see, nevertheless, looking at other nurseries gives you an idea of the range of nursery care on offer. Nurseries come in all shapes and sizes, and without visiting a few, you will have no idea what will best suit your needs.

Telephone and make an appointment. Nurseries are busy places, and arriving unannounced is probably not a good idea. Spend some time talking to the person in charge, as well as having a good look around. Go when children are in the nursery, so you can see how staff and children respond to one another. Another unannounced visit would be a good idea before making a final decision.

Twenty questions to ask in a nursery

Some answers to the following questions may be included in the information sent by the nursery. Of course, some questions may not be appropriate – if you are looking for a place for your 3- year-old, finding out how they feed babies won't be of interest! On the other hand, if you are looking for a baby place, remember that your infant will move through the different age groups if they stay in the nursery. These questions are also set out in Box 10.1, which you can use as a checklist.

Information box 10.1: Checklist for assessing a nursery

Twenty questions to ask in a nursery

1	Who owns and runs the nursery?	OK	Not sure
2	What are the nursery's aims and objectives?	OK	Not sure
3	How many staff have been trained to care for children?	OK	Not sure
4	How are students and people on youth training programmes used?	OK	Not sure
5	How many children are there per member of staff?	OK	Not sure
6	How long do staff usually stay?	OK	Not sure
7	Who will be caring for my child?	OK	Not sure
8	What happens when staff are away?	OK	Not sure
9	Does the nursery employ domestic staff?	OK	Not sure
10	How are mealtimes handled?	OK	Not sure
11	What is your policy on feeding babies?	OK	Not sure
12	How is the day organized?	OK	Not sure
13	What is your policy on parental involvement?	OK	Not sure

14	How is information shared with parents?	OK	Not sure
15	Do you have a settling-in policy?	OK	Not sure
16	What is your policy on discipline?	OK	Not sure
17	How flexible are your opening times?	OK	Not sure
18	What is your policy on sick children?	OK	Not sure
19	Fees?	OK	Not sure
20	Special needs?	OK	Not sure

Ten things to look for

1	Is the nursery clean, safe and bright?	OK	Not sure
2	Is there enough space for children to play?	OK	Not sure
3	What's the toilet area like?	OK	Not sure
4	Where do children rest?	OK	Not sure
5	Are there cozy, comfortable areas where children can relax?	OK	Not sure
6	Is there a range and generous supply of toys and equipment?	OK	Not sure
7	Is there evidence that they value cultural differences?	OK	Not sure
8	Are infant chairs, etc., used appropriately?	OK	Not sure

9	Do staff seem to have a warm and caring relationship with the children?	OK	Not sure
10	Do children seem happy, content and involved in what they are doing?	OK	Not sure

Twenty questions to ask in a nursery

1   *Who owns and runs the nursery?* It helps to know how often the owner of the nursery is around and how much responsibility the officer-in-charge has for making decisions. Does the nursery have a management committee? Are parents included? Allowing parents a say in the management of the nursery suggests that the nursery will respond to their needs and views.

2   *What are the nursery's aims and objectives?* Knowing what the nursery wants to offer children and their families will help you decide whether it can provide what you want for your child.

3   *How many staff have been trained to care for children?* Does the head of the nursery have a relevant qualification, such as an NNEB? How well qualified are other members of staff? Some nurseries have trained teachers working with older children.

4   *How are students and people on youth training programmes used?* These people are in the nursery as part of their training. They can play a valuable role, but they should not be used to replace permanent or trained staff. Some nurseries put students in situations they're not trained to deal with – for example, taking sole charge of a group of children.

5   *How many children are there per member of staff?* This will vary
    depending on the age of the children in the group. There
    should be more staff for younger children – at least one adult
    to every three babies, and one to five for older children. Be
    sure to ask about each group. Ask whom they include in the
    adult–child ratio. Some nurseries include students and
    trainees in their ratios – because they often lack experience
    and training, this is not good practice.

6   *How long do staff usually stay?* How many staff have left in the
    last year? Also ask how long the officer-in-charge has been at
    the nursery. This will tell you something about both staff
    turnover and working conditions – staff are unlikely to stay
    when conditions are poor.

7   *Who will be caring for my child?* Children tend to do better and
    settle more easily when the same carer looks after them.
    Check whether the nursery has a key worker system, and ask
    how this works. How do children know who their key worker
    is? How many staff in the group are full-time? Using a num-
    ber of part-time staff can mean that children have different
    carers at different times of the day.

8   *What happens when staff are away?* Does someone come in to
    cover for the absent person? Is cover provided by the same
    person each time? From the children's point of view, it is
    better if temporary cover is provided by someone they are
    familiar with.

9   *Does the nursery employ domestic staff?* This may seem a
    strange question. However, if childcare staff have to clean
    and cook too, they will have less time to spend with chil-
    dren.

10   *How are mealtimes handled?* Not all nurseries provide cooked meals. Where they do, find out the sort of food they dish up. Ask to see the week's menu – does it seem a healthy diet? How are mealtimes organized? What do staff do when a child refuses to eat their dinner?

11   *What is your policy on feeding babies?* Continuing breast-feeding can be difficult once you are back at work. Success depends as much on the attitudes of nursery staff as on you and your work situation. How do staff react if you want to continue breast-feeding when your child is at the nursery? Is there a comfortable place for you to use?

12   *How is the day organized?* What do children do at different times of the day? Are there a variety of play activities each day? Do children play outside? Do children watch television? If so, when and what do they watch?

13   *What is your policy on parental involvement?* Are parents welcomed into the nursery? Can they drop in any time? Are parents encouraged to stay at drop-off or pick-up times?

14   *How is information about children and the nursery shared with parents?* When parents and carers talk frequently with each other, everyone – including the children – feels better about childcare. Ask whether staff have time to talk to parents at arrival and collection times. Look for other examples of sharing information, such as child reviews, newsletters, diaries, a suggestion box, a notice board and open days or evenings.

15   *Do you have a settling-in policy?* Is there a gradual introduction to the nursery? Is a parent or familiar adult encouraged to stay until the child has settled? What do they do when a child is crying for their parents?

16 *What is your policy on discipline?* What are the rules for children? Are they reasonable, given the age and ability of children in the group? What do staff do when children fight over toys? How do they handle temper trantrums? Do all staff respond in a similar way?

17 *How flexible are your opening times?* What happens if you are a little late collecting your child?

18 *What is your policy on sick children?* Do they have a sick bay? Will they give medicines?

19 *Fees?* Do you have to pay if your child is absent due to holidays or illness? How often are fees reviewed?

20 *Special needs?* If your child has special needs, you will want to make sure that the nursery has staff who will understand their needs. Many nurseries can call on specialist help for children with special needs.

Ask to be shown around the nursery. Make sure you see all areas, not just those that your child will be using. Remember, your baby will move to toddler and preschool rooms eventually. Ask if you can spend a little time watching in each room – this will give you a good feel for what life is like in the nursery and how staff behave.

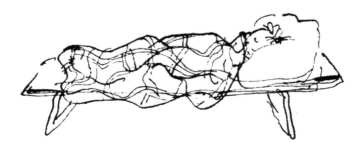

A brief tour of the nursery won't tell you everything. Only by spending time watching staff and children can you really know what goes on. Most nurseries are not used to parents making such a request, and they may be reluctant to agree. They may claim that having a strange adult in the room will upset the children. In fact, children are rarely upset by someone else being in the room – it's usually the staff who feel uncomfortable.

What do I need to look for?

Some nurseries have purpose-built accommodation, but many are less fortunate. It's common to find nurseries in converted houses, church or community halls, scout huts or offices. Most, but not all, nurseries in converted accommodation are on the ground floor. Some nurseries have to share buildings with other users. Where sharing goes on, staff may have to pack up nursery equipment at the end of every day, only to set it up again the following morning – clearly, this is not an ideal situation. Whatever accommodation it has, a nursery should be clean, safe and welcoming. Here are a few things to look out for as they show you around. They are also included as a checklist in Box 10.1.

1   *Is the nursery clean, safe and bright?* Does the nursery seem well kept and regularly cleaned? Is there enough natural light? Check that there are no safety hazards. Is the front door kept locked?

2   *Is there enough space for children to play without getting in each other's way?* If there is little storage space, the room may be cluttered with furniture and equipment, which may leave very little clear floor space for playing. Is there a safe outside play space? If the nursery does not have its own space, ask if

they take the children out, and where they go. How often do children go out? Is there a range of equipment for outside play?

3 *What's the toilet area like?* Is it clean and free of smells? Are the toilets and basins child-sized? Are individual towels or paper towels provided? Is water limited to safe a temperature?

4 *Where do children rest?* Is there enough space for the number of children? Resting is not easy for children if the space is cramped. Does the atmosphere encourage sleep/rest (for example, dimly-lit, good ventilation, quiet, cots, mattresses or beds)?

5 *Are there cozy, comfortable areas where children can relax?* The nursery day can be a long one. It helps if the room has some soft areas where children can relax and take time out from play activities – having a book corner with a rug and cushions is one example. Some nurseries have a sofa, large comfortable chairs or big floor cushions on which to curl up.

6 *Is there a range and generous supply of toys and equipment?* Ask them to show you the toys and equipment if they are not out. Is there a variety of play things? For example, in the baby room you might see soft toys, rattles and shakers, nesting and stacking toys, picture books, push and pull toys, large balls, mobiles and mirrors. Babies need a wide range of textures and shapes to explore with their hands and mouth. Check that the toys and play equipment are in good repair. There should be enough equipment for the number of children in the group.

7   *Is there evidence that they value cultural differences?* Do wall displays, toys and equipment (for example, books, stories, puzzles, pretend play props) show people and events from a range of cultures?

8   *Are infant chairs, high chairs, play pens, walkers and cots used appropriately?* Babies need to be held a lot, and they also need to be able to explore their surroundings, as do toddlers. Keeping infants and toddlers in this sort of equipment for too long, whether happy or not, is not a good idea – their movements are restricted, and using such equipment (apart from mealtimes) does not encourage interactions between staff and child.

9   *Do staff seem to have a warm and caring relationship with the children?* Do children seem comfortable around staff? Do they come to them for help, comfort or reassurance? How do staff talk to children?

10   *Do children seem happy, content and involved in what they are doing?* Children shouldn't be bored, be staring vacantly into space, be wandering around with nothing to do, or unnaturally quiet. Nor should they look miserable or afraid. Watch to see if children are hesitant or look nervously at staff when they are playing. This behaviour might suggest that staff are too strict.

Having made all your checks, you have to decide whether this is a suitable nursery to leave your child. If you are unhappy about anything, try to sort it out with the nursery. If you still feel unsure, it's probably best not to continue with the place.

Finalizing the arrangement – signing a contract

Having decided this nursery is for you, and having put your child's name on the waiting list, you may have to wait some time before a place is available. If this is the case, visiting the nursery again to check that there has been no major change is probably wise. Before your child starts, you will want to find out more about the settling-in procedure. More information on settling in can be found in Chapter 11. Agreeing and signing a contract is important. Although it refers to childminders, much of the information in Box 9.3 (see page 111) is relevant to nurseries.

11
Making childcare work

You may think your problems are over once you have found a place and signed a contract, yet this is only the beginning. Childcare is a partnership between providers, children and parents. Obtaining good quality childcare depends on all those involved maintaining good relationships. As with any relationship, it requires effort to make it work to everyone's satisfaction. In this chapter, we offer a few hints on how to develop and maintain a successful working relationship with those providing care for your child

Communication is often the key to a successful partnership. Parents, children and carers feel more positive about childcare experiences when parents and carers talk to each other regularly. Encourage childminders or nursery staff to tell you what your child has been doing during the day – you can respond by telling them about what has been happening at home. Some providers encourage communication by keeping diaries or notebooks that they fill in each day and then give to parents to take home. Information of this kind helps both you and your childcarer to understand your child's behaviour.

Arrange a regular time to share information if possible. It may not be easy – in the mornings, you may be in a hurry to get to work, and childminders might have children to take to school; in the evenings, you probably want to get home as quickly as possible, and childminders want time to spend with their family too. Nursery staff are sometimes busy with other children, though they should still make time to chat with parents. Although you don't have to spend a long time talking, there are other ways to overcome the problem of time and convenience. Organizing a regular time or making an appointment obviously helps, and it also shows the provider that you recognize that their time is as valuable as yours.

Do talk to your carer if something is bothering you. Parents often worry about raising issues with care providers. Many feel that if they complain, their childcare provider will not want to look after their child any longer. This situation seems more common among parents using childminders rather than nurseries. Nurseries often have someone in charge with whom you can discuss a problem, which makes it a little easier. However, letting a problem develop into a situation that becomes even more difficult to sort out is not going to be beneficial from anyone's point of view. When you get around to talking, remember that with any problem, there are usually two points of view – yours and the carer's.

Another thing that's worth bearing in mind is that whoever you get to look after your child, they are not your double – however much you would like them to be, they are different from you and, in particular situations, will react differently. That's why it's important that the relationship between yourself and your child's carer is based on mutual trust and respect

Being considerate will help make any partnership work. Nobody likes being taken for granted, particularly at work. In particular, try to remember that although childminders are at home, they are

still working. Childminders sometimes feel that parents take advantage of this situation by not being as punctual as they might. When people are busy, their behaviour sometimes appears thoughtless. Allow time for some polite conversation with your childcare provider. Get to know the names of nursery staff, and greet them when you arrive. Show your appreciation when it is due. These kinds of things make people feel valued.

Care providers don't make too many complaints about inconsiderate parents, but when they do complain, it's usually about the same four problems:

1   *Payment* – Pay fees on time. No one finds it acceptable if their employer makes them wait for their money, and childcare providers are no different. Many ask parents to pay a week in advance, partly to avoid problems of non-payment. Remember that a provider will need to review and increase fees over time. You should cover these points in your contract.

2   *Timekeeping* – Keep to your agreed drop-off and pick-up times. Obviously, there will be times when you are unavoidably delayed – the train was cancelled, the traffic was bad, the meeting ran on. Providers will usually be sympathetic in these situations, and more so if you have already agreed to pay overtime in such circumstances. If you do know you are going to be late, ring and let the nursery or childminder know – this avoids worry, upset and irritation for everyone. It is not fair on either your childcare provider or your child to arrive early or late on a regular basis. Good nurseries and childminders plan activities, and early or late arrivals can play havoc with timetables. If necessary, renegotiate drop-off and pick-up times. Otherwise, you should be prepared to pay overtime.

3   *Illness* – If your child is unwell, ring and discuss the situation with the nursery or childminder *before turning up*. Some employers are not sympathetic towards women who need time off to be with a sick child. The temptation to take your child to the nursery or childminder in the hope that they will accept the child can be strong. Though very understandable, this is not a good idea – if your child is really unwell, the provider is unlikely to be able to give them the care and attention that a sick child needs. If they are infectious, they may pass the illness on to others, including the provider herself. We give more thought to managing such a crisis later in this chapter.

4   *Clothing* – This may seem obvious, but it's not very practical to dress children in their best clothes. Even with aprons, clothes can be splashed with paint, etc. Giving your child outdoor clothing suitable for our weather is also essential! Carers often complain about children arriving inadequately dressed for the day. It may also be a good idea to put name labels on more expensive items of your child's clothing – mistakes can occur when five children have identical coats.

Settling in

The first few days of a new childcare place can be very difficult for children. The early days can be hard for parents as well – it's what psychologists call 'separation anxiety'. It doesn't affect everybody, but many parents and children experience some anxiety. Research has led nurseries, schools, hospitals and playgroups to change their practices in recent years.

Slowly easing a child into a new place is without doubt the best way of keeping any upset to a minimum. The happier the child, the quicker they establish good relationships with adults looking after them. You will feel much more confident about leaving your child if they are happy and settled. Don't be taken in by those who say the old-fashioned way of making a quick, clean break is best – it isn't.

Usually, settling in involves you spending time with your child in the nursery or with the childminder. You can gradually reduce the time each day until you think your child will be happy left alone. This time is also useful for you and the carer, enabling you to get to know each other and learn about each other's routines with respect to your child. It's a fact that no matter how well you manage the settling-in process, some children will still be upset when it's time for you to go – talk to nursery staff or your child-minder about the best way to handle this situation.

Key workers

In Chapter 6, we talked about key workers – this system involves nurseries assigning a particular member of staff to look after a small group of children. At times like settling-in periods, having a key worker can make things very much easier. Nurseries will often alter a key worker's usual duties to take account of the extra time involved in settling in a new child. Although your child is in new and strange surroundings, at least the same familiar person always looks after them, and you have someone you can turn to for help and advice should the need arise.

Home visits

To help with settling in, a few nurseries will now arrange for a member of staff to visit you at home. A home visit gives the nursery worker a chance to meet you and your child in a familiar setting. First impressions are important – if staff have only ever seen your child upset and anxious about being in the nursery for the first time, it can create a false impression. A home visit also gives your child a chance to get to know the carer on their own territory. Of course, home visits are not convenient for everybody – you may prefer to meet in the nursery. Nevertheless, remember, having the choice is no bad thing. If you are using a childminder, you could invite her to visit you at home too.

How long will it take to settle my child?

Children, parents, nurseries and childminders are all different. Some children will settle quite quickly, other children may find it very hard to adjust. You may be able to spend several days settling your child, but if you are working full-time, you may not. If time is a problem for you, perhaps another close relative or friend could help. What your child needs at this stage is a familiar face. Try to start settling in your child before you return to work, then, if it does take longer, you will have the necessary time.

Whatever the situations you are faced with, there are several things you can do to prepare the ground, and Box 11.1 contains a few useful suggestions.

Preparing yourself for the separation

Just as children need to get used to a new childcare arrangement, it's as well to remember that parents often have to get used to the idea of leaving their child with someone else.

Mothers – though rarely fathers – sometimes feel that because they will not be spending most of their time with their children, they will be harming them in some way. This is an understandable worry, and it stems from the misplaced belief that children need full-time care from their mothers in order to develop normally. There is no research evidence to support this view – how children develop is not directly linked to whether their mothers are with them most of the time or not.

Information box 11.1: Settling your child into a new childcare place

- Give the care provider information about:

  - your child's nickname
  - toilet habits
  - favourite toys
  - daily routines
  - food likes and dislikes

- Agree on a settling-in plan.
- Talk to your child about the nursery or childminder.
- Tell your child where you are going and when you will be back.
- Don't drag out leaving – cuddle, say goodbye and leave.
- Don't try to creep out unnoticed.
- Take a favourite toy from home for your child to play with.
- Leave something personal of your own for your child to keep.
- Make sure the care provider has contact telephone numbers for you.
- Tell the provider about recent events at home.
- Provide spare clothing in case of accidents.
- Try not to introduce changes at home.

Another common fear is that your child will become closer to the childcare provider than to you, because they spend so much time with them. This leads some mothers to choose a nursery rather than a childminder – they feel there is less chance that their child will get too attached to one person.

There are two important points to bear in mind. Firstly, children can and do have close relationships with many adults, including their childminder, nursery worker or nanny. As we have

said before, having close relationships with other people is important for children's development. Secondly, being close to their
carer does not affect their close bond with their parents – for
example, Israeli children raised in a kibbutz form their strongest
bonds with their parents, despite spending most of the time with
other adults. However many, or few, the hours spent with your
child, it is the *quality* of the interactions between the two of you
which is important for close attachments, not the *amount of time*
you spend together.

Coming and going

Children sometimes play up at handing-over times. When you
arrive in the morning, they say they don't want to stay, and get
upset when you leave. When you come to pick them up, they may
misbehave and refuse to go home. Children will play up at different times – they may be fine about coming, but difficult about
going, or vice versa. If this situation does arise, despite having
spent time settling in, it could be a phase your child is going
through – children have their ups and downs, just like adults.

This sort of behaviour is often difficult to handle. It can be upsetting, particularly if it involves lots of crying or tantrums. Parents can feel bad if it seems as though their offspring prefers the carer to them. Don't ignore the problem. It usually helps to keep to the same routine when you leave your child. Spending a little time settling them with a book, toy or playmate before leaving often works well. Try to avoid a rushed and hurried goodbye. However, there will be times when you can't avoid this. Don't be tempted to creep out unnoticed – a sudden disappearance can be very frightening for a child.

By far the best thing to do is talk to the provider about the best way to handle the situation – she is almost certain to have encountered this sort of thing before. It's definitely important to agree who is in charge when both of you are present – children are quick to take advantage of confusion.

Sometimes, being difficult at drop-off or pick-up times comes out of the blue. The child has, up to this point, been settled, and coming and going has been OK. Talking to the carer will help you to work out if something has happened to cause the sudden change, or whether it is a phase the child is going through – it could be both!

A child who protests at handing-over times may be trying to tell you that all is not well. You should obviously check things out. Alternatively, it could be an attempt to control the adults. Children can work out that if they make a fuss, parents won't go. If you suspect this to be the case, talk it over with the carer, decide how far it will go, and who will take charge. Finally, the protests – whatever form they take – may have nothing to do with the child-care situation – they may be about something else, and the distress only shows itself at coming and going times.

Monitoring progress

While your child is in childcare, you will need to monitor their progress regularly. Check that all is well and that they are developing to the best of their ability. Nurseries and childminders who offer good quality care will make a point of discussing your child's progress regularly – in this way, they spot any problems quickly and, if necessary, seek help. If you are concerned that your child is falling behind, discuss it with the provider and also your health visitor or GP. It's also advisable to keep an eye on behaviour and health at home. Look out for new problems, such as bedwetting, loss of appetite, nightmares, aggressive behaviour, tantrums, sadness or lack of interest. Some reaction from children is to be expected to begin with – your child is adjusting to a whole new world. During this period, they need you to be as reassuring and patient as possible. Letting the carer know what's happening and talking it over with them will help too. However, if the problem continues and you believe it is directly related to childcare, you will need to consider whether a change is called for. If you are worried, but are not sure if it is justified, talk it over with someone such as a friend, health visitor or childcare adviser first.

Managing a crisis

It is inevitable that a crisis will arise sooner or later. Hopefully, it will not be a major one. Nevertheless, it is a good idea to be prepared. Illness is the major problem for most parents. Children often come down with several minor illnesses when they first start nursery, because they are more vulnerable to infections, and it takes a while for them to build up resistance. If you are going back to work, try to establish a network of support in case of emergencies – for example, a friend, relative or close neighbour who may be able to step in and help. Although you probably cannot return the favour if you work full-time, maybe you can offer to help them out in other ways, such as inviting their children to tea or on a visit at the weekend.

Where to go for help when it's not working to your satisfaction

Naturally, the first place to begin with is the childminder or nursery. Raising matters that are bothering you can sometimes seem easier in a nursery, because there is a staff group and a person in charge. However, whether using a childminder or nursery, talking is important. Very often, situations get out of hand or misunderstandings arise because we don't tell those involved how we feel. You may find it helpful to talk to someone else – for example, you could contact one of the national organizations listed in 'Useful organizations', or an under-eights adviser. You may want to talk to other parents using the facility if you think the problem is something which affects them too.

Changing childcare

We have already stressed the importance of stability of care – too many changes can affect children's development. Consequently, trying to work through and resolve any problems that do crop up is better than moving the child at the first sign of trouble. However, if the arrangement is not working out, despite doing your best to make it work, making a change is better than continuing with an unsatisfactory situation. Keeping a child in a poor setting can be more damaging than making a move.

And finally . . .

We have written this book to help you in your search for good quality childcare. We hope that having read it, you know more about what quality childcare means. Of course, quality, as we have said before, means different things to different people. Many childcare providers you visit  won't be doing *all* the things we have covered in these chapters. You will need to make some compromises. Now that you've read the book, you should be in a position to decide what is important to you.

Having read about what good childcare consists of, you may have had a few thoughts about your abilities as a parent. Do you always do all the right things? Of course not. But there again, you are a parent, not a professional childcarer – there is a difference. As a parent you need to be realistic when making comparisons between your childcare skills and the professionals. Just because you don't spend every minute of your spare time getting the paints out or sticking bits of pasta together for your children doesn't mean you are inadequate as a parent.

You may find yourself in a situation where you simply can't find a provider who matches up to your standards. Don't despair! We recognize that not every parent has a large choice when it comes to good quality childcare – some parents would argue that they have no choice at all. However, it's worth remembering that parents are the customers when it comes to childcare.

Parents who know about quality in childcare can help raise standards by asking providers the kinds of questions set out in this book. As more parents make their demands known, so quality will improve. Each of us has an important part to play in improving childcare standards. The pay-off will be enormous – especially for our children.

Useful organizations

This is not a complete list of all organizations working in the field of childcare. *Free to Work: A Guide to Childcare in England and Wales,* by P. Kavanagh-Mosson and C. Burke (Gingerbread, 1994), lists both national and local organizations and contacts, and is sold through J. Sainsbury's.

Aids Education and Research Trust (AVERT)
11 Denne Parade
Horsham
West Sussex RH12 1JD
Tel: 01403 210202

British Association for Early Childhood Education (BAECE)
111 City View House
463 Bethnal Green Road
London E2 9QY
Tel: 0171 739 7594

Campaigning organization for nursery provision and day care. Local groups.

Child Accident Prevention Trust
28 Portland Place
London W1N 4DE
Tel: 0171 636 2545

Information for parents, carers and local authorities on how to prevent child accidents.

Daycare Trust/National Child Care Campaign
Wesley House
4 Wild Court
London WC2B 5AU
Tel: 0171 405 5617

Campaigns for child care provision nationally. Provides information about finding good quality childcare. Publishes quarterly magazine.

Citizens' Advice Bureau

Check your local telephone directory for your nearest branch.

Department for Education and Employment
Sanctuary Buildings
Great Smith Street
London SW1P 3BT
Tel: 0171 925 5000
Tel: 0345 543345 (helpline for nursery vouchers – charged at local call rates)

Equal Opportunities Commission
Overseas House
Quay Street
Manchester M3 3HN
Tel: 0161 733 9244

Gingerbread
16–17 Clerkenwell Close
London EC1R 0AA
Tel: 0171 336 8183

A network of support groups for single parents and their children.
Free telephone advice service.

Kids' Clubs Network
Belleriv House
3 Muirfield Crescent
London E14 9SZ
Tel: 0171 512 2212

Promotes out of school care for school aged children. Maintains a
directory of all out of school clubs in the UK. Local branches.

Letterbox Library
8 Bradbury Street
London N16 8JN
Tel: 0171 254 1640

Supplies multicultural, non-sexist, environmentally aware books
for children. Also produces a newsletter for subscribers.

**National Association of Toy and Leisure Libraries (Play
Matters)**
68 Churchway
London NW1 1LT
Tel: 0171 387 9592

Publishes annual *Good Toy Guide* and brief guides, such as *Play
For All*, *Talk To Me*, *Mucky Play*, *Do It Yourself* and *Toys and Child
Development*.

National Childminding Association
8 Masons Hill
Bromley
Kent BR2 9EY
Tel: 0181 464 6164

Supports childminders in their work. Publishes information for parents about childminding.

National Children's Bureau
8 Wakley Street
London EC1V 7QE
Tel: 0171 278 9441

Information, training and advice on child-related matters, including daycare and preschool provision.

National Council for One Parent Families
255 Kentish Town Road
London NW5 2LX
Tel: 0171 267 1361

Advice and information for lone parents.

National Early Years Network
77 Holloway Road
London N7 8JZ
Tel: 0171 607 9573

Provides a platform for developing ideas on provision for young children. Circulates information on relevant issues.

National Playbus Association
AMF House
Whitby Road
Brislington
Bristol BS43QF
Tel: 0117 9775375

Provides details of local playbus associations.

New Ways to Work
309 Upper Street
London N1 2TY
Tel: 0171 226 4026

Information on flexible working arrangements. Free newsletter to members.

Parents at Work
45 Beech Street
London EC2Y 8AD
Tel: 0171 628 3578 (helpline)

Advice and information for working parents. Local groups.

Pre-School Learning Alliance (previously Pre-school Playgroups Association – PPA)
61–63 King's Cross Road
London WC1X 9LL
Tel: 0171 833 0991

Advice and information about playgroups throughout the UK.

Step by Step
Unit 4, Brunel Way
Thornbury Industrial Estate
Thornbury
Bristol BS12 2NR
Tel: 01454 281200

Mail-order supplier of preschool equipment and materials. Multi-cultural resource collection includes dolls, puppets, playpeople, tray puzzles, cards, books and posters.

Working Group Against Racism in Children's Resources
460 Wandsworth Road
London SW8 3LX
Tel: 0171 627 4594

Provides guidelines for evaluating and selecting children's toys and other resources.

Further reading

Aids Education and Research Trust (1992) *Aids and Children: What's It Got To Do With Them?*, Horsham, West Sussex: AVERT.

British Association for Early Childhood Education (1994) *Play – The Key to Young Children's Learning*, London: BAECE.

Child Accident Prevention Trust (1992) *Accident Prevention in Day Care and Play Settings: A Practical Guide*, London: CAPT and N.E.S Arnold Educational Suppliers.

Department of Education and Science (1990) *Starting with Quality: Report of Committee of Inquiry*, London: HMSO.

Department of Health (1991) *The Children Act 1989, Guidance and Regulations, Volume 2: Family Support, Day Care and Educational Provision for Young Children*, London: HMSO.

Equal Opportunities Commission (1992) *An Equal Start: Guidelines on Equal Treatment for the Under Eights*, London: EOC.

Health Education Authority (undated) *Play It Safe! A Guide to Preventing Children's Accidents*, London: HEA.

E. Hennessy, S. Martin, P. Moss and E. Melhuish (1992) *Children and Day Care: Lessons from Research*, London: Paul Chapman.

P. Kavanagh-Mosson and C. Burke (1994) *Free to Work: A Guide to Childcare in England and Wales*, London: Gingerbread.

P. Moss and E. Melhuish (1991) *Current Issues in Day Care for Young Children*, London: HMSO.

National Childminding Association (1992) *Setting the Standards: Guidelines on Good Practice in Registering Childminders*, London: NCMA.

National Childminding Association (1993) *The Key to Quality*, London: NCMA.

National Children's Bureau (1990) *Babies and Toddlers: Carers and Educators: Quality for the Under Threes*, London: NCB.

D.A. Phillips (1987) *Quality in Child Care: What Does Research Tell Us?* Washington, DC: National Association for the Education of Young Children.

Richard C. Woolfson (1993) *An A-Z of Child Development*, London: Souvenir Press.

Index